The Magic Pill

By **T.J. Rohleder**
(a.k.a "The Blue Jeans Millionaire")

TABLE OF CONTENTS

Introduction:

By T.J. Rohleder

The Magic Secret to Dramatically Increasing Your Sales and Profits!

Congratulations on your decision to read this book. This separates you from all of the other entrepreneurs and small businesspeople who 'claim' they want to make more money, but won't take the time to study a book that can help them do it.

Yes, so many people want the MAJOR BENEFITS of being in business — without going through all of the time, work, and effort to get them. This is true in all aspects of life. People want THE VERY BEST RESULTS, but don't want to pay the price to get them. **And that's sad because business has SO MANY GREAT REWARDS TO OFFER!** It can lead to a life of complete and total freedom and fulfillment. And finding all of the ways and means to make more money can be a great deal of fun!

So what's the secret? That's simple, just become A GREAT MARKETER. This is the key to dramatically increasing your sales and profits. It's the secret that gives you a MAJOR UNFAIR ADVANTAGE over all of your competitors... And once you get good at marketing yourself and your business, you'll discover that...

THIS IS THE GREATEST GAME ON EARTH!

Not only can learning how to become a great marketer make you a lot of money, but it's also VERY REWARDING and a lot of fun!

<u>Marketing</u> <u>is</u> <u>made</u> <u>up</u> <u>of</u> **<u>all</u> <u>the</u> <u>things</u> <u>you</u> <u>do</u> <u>to</u> <u>ATTRACT</u> <u>and</u> <u>RETAIN</u> <u>the</u> <u>largest</u> <u>number</u> <u>of</u> <u>the</u> <u>very</u> <u>best</u> <u>prospective</u> <u>buyers</u>** <u>in</u> <u>your</u> <u>market</u>. That's it. It sounds simple because it is! Of course, like everything else that's most worthwhile, IT'S NOT EASY. This is especially true in today's overcrowded and over-hyped marketplace. But tell me ANY GAME that's easy and I'll show you one boring game that you don't want to play!

Anyway, the fact that learning how to become a great marketer is difficult is THE #1 REASON why none of your competitors will EVER do it. Remember that. Think deeply about that. Then consider this fact: **Your ability to ATTRACT and RETAIN the very best customers in your marketplace is the key to making all the money you've ever dreamed of making.** Sure, there's a learning curve you must go through and it can be a bit painful. But that's THE PRICE you must continually pay to get really good at ANYTHING you want bad enough. And I promise, when you get good at all of the things you have to do to MARKET YOURSELF AND YOUR BUSINESS, you'll have a major, unfair advantage over all of the people and companies who are also trying to do business with the same prospects and customers that you're trying to attract and retain.

So please **let this be your #1 FOCUS** as you go through

this book. Have fun reading and thinking about all of the powerful ideas and strategies I'm about to share with you.

Here's What You'll Discover In This Book

This book gives you 17 of my most powerful marketing secrets that I've used to generate millions of dollars in my own business. The first chapter is also the title of this book. It tells you how to dramatically INCREASE YOUR SALES AND PROFITS by giving your customers what I call *'The Magic Pill.'* As you'll see, **this 'Magic Pill' is the powerful combination of products and services [and offers] that your very best prospects and customers want more than anything else.** This is made up of all of the things they BADLY WANT and are NOT getting anywhere else. When you find and develop these *'Magic Pills'* — ALL of the very best prospective buyers in your marketplace will practically stand in line with money in hand and beg you to take it!

HOW'S THAT for a great visual!

As you know, every business exists to serve its marketplace. And yet, how many entrepreneurs and business owners are TOTALLY FOCUSED on giving their best prospects and customers THE ONE THING that they want more than anything else and are not getting from any other competitor? Very few, IF ANY!!! But you can and WILL when you simply do the things that I tell you about in Chapter One. So go through this first chapter right away and discover the secrets to developing your own *'Magic Pills'* that can completely TRANSFORM YOUR BUSINESS. As you'll see, **this gives you a very real 'unfair advantage' over the other people and**

companies who are trying to do business with the same people you're after. I'll go over all the details you need in Chapter One. I sincerely hope you'll use these secrets to create your own 'Magic Pills' that will make it MUCH EASIER for you to attract and retain the very best prospects and customers. Please go over this chapter and then go through the rest of this book to discover some of my other marketing secrets that can help you dramatically increase your sales and profits.

And to reward you for purchasing this book, I have…

A great FREE business-building gift for you!

Yes, I have a gift waiting for you that can DRAMATICALLY INCREASE YOUR SALES AND PROFITS! Here's what it's all about: I spent TEN FULL YEARS writing down all of the greatest marketing and success secrets I discovered during that time period. Each day, I took a few notes and, at the end of a decade, I had a GIANT LIST of 6,159 powerful secrets! This list is ALMOST 1,000 PAGES of hard core money-making ideas and strategies!** **Best of all, this massive collection is now YOURS ABSOLUTELY FREE!** Just go to: www.6159FreeSecrets.com and get it NOW! As you'll see, this complete collection of 6,159 of my greatest marketing and success secrets, far more valuable than those you can buy from others for $495 to $997, is absolutely **FREE.** No cost, no obligation.

Why am I giving away this GIANT COLLECTION of secrets, that took ONE DECADE to discover and compile, FOR FREE? That's simple: I believe many of the people who receive these 6,159 secrets in this huge 955 page PDF document will want to obtain some of our other books and audio programs and participate in our special COACHING PROGRAMS. However, you are NOT obligated to buy anything—now or ever.

I know you're serious about making more money or you wouldn't be reading this. So go to: www.6159FreeSecrets.com and get this complete collection of 6,159 of my greatest marketing and success secrets right now! **You'll get this GREAT FREE GIFT in the next few minutes, just for letting me add you to my Client mailing list,** and I'll stay in CLOSE TOUCH with you… and do all I can to help you make even more money with my proven marketing strategies and methods.

So with all this said, let's begin…

** WARNING: This complete collection of 6,159 marketing and success secrets contains MANY CONTROVERSIAL ideas and methods. Also, it was originally written for MY EYES ONLY and for a few VERY CLOSE FRIENDS. Therefore, the language is X-RATED in some places [I got VERY EXCITED when I wrote many of these ideas and used VERY FOUL LANGUAGE to get my ideas across!] so 'IF' you are EASILY OFFENDED or do NOT want to read anything OFFENSIVE, then please do both of us a favor and DO NOT go to my website and download this FREE gift. THANK YOU for your understanding.

CHAPTER ONE

People are looking for and willing to spend a ton of money for:

The Magic Pill!

This is the product or service that they perceive can instantly and automatically give them something they badly want.

The Magic Pill

Here's one reality of business that you need to both accept and take advantage of if you want to succeed: **everyone in your marketplace is looking for a Magic Pill. Everyone.** No one wants to go through the pain of tearing yourself down before you can build yourself up again, and the same is true of any form of pain. **People don't want to go through any pain to achieve results.**

So look for the Magic Pill—the product or service that the people in your marketplace *think* can instantly and automatically give them something they badly want. They're looking for this Magic Pill right now, and they're willing to spend a ton of money to get it. **If you can give it to them, the money is going to rain down on your head.** People are going to stand in line with money in hand to buy it, because it's very exciting to them—something that turns them on more than anything else. It's that "wow factor": it captivates their imagination. **It contains the biggest benefit they're looking for, with the least possible amount of headaches and hassles. That's what makes it a Magic Pill.**

My Marketing Director, Chris Lakey, recently came up with an idea that's way outside of the box—something that I never thought of, in fact. It's a way that we can potentially give our pet boutique customers something that nobody else gives them a way that we can take away some of the headaches and hassles they normally have to deal with, especially if we're able to combine it with the idea that I talked about earlier. That is, we're hoping to mix it with a free service that they're currently spending money for. **The idea is to go to their house and do their work for them.** They don't have to do anything except be home at a certain time. **So they get the very biggest benefit that they're looking for the most, and they get it for free— although there *is* a little condition that they have to understand right up front.**

We're taking away all the headaches and hassles, and those are the kinds of things that can potentially give you that Magic Pill. The Pill will vary from business to business, because of course every business is different. How do you find the Magic Pill? **Well, it starts with a deep understanding of what it is that your customers are looking for, which takes the kind of intimate knowledge you develop during the relationship-building aspect of your business.** Pay close attention to what people are doing. Look at what your customers are buying right now, and follow the money like a good detective. What are the number one benefits they're looking for? Why are they spending their money?

Look for all the headaches and hassles they're facing and work to take them away. Give them what they want, without any of the pain that they'd normally have to go through to get it, and then just stand back. We've actually done this perfectly at M.O.R.E., Inc. once or twice. **At the end of one sales presentation, for example, we actually got stampeded.** Not only did people want the product bad enough to immediately pull out their checkbooks and credit cards, they actually stormed the stage—to the point where some of our staff people got knocked over! One of our guys got pushed over and had his finger broken by an otherwise very fine, rational, meek and mild-mannered customer who became an animal because we offered him what he really wanted!

That's when you know you've got a Magic Pill: when people stampede you in person, or when instead of sending their orders in by regular mail, they spend an extra $30-50 to get them in by Federal Express. Or they get in their cars and drive the order across three states to get it to you more quickly. **When you test something and you get three or four times the normal response that you'd normally get, *then* you know you have the Magic Pill. This is the reward for all of the hard work!** Look, none of this is easy; if this book has a unifying theme, that's it. And yet when you constantly strive to find that right combination of products and services that just totally drives people crazy, you'll make so much money so fast that you'll wonder where it all was before!

And I'll *tell* you where it all was. It was in the bank accounts and credit card authorizations and the available lines of credit of all of the people in your market... but until then, you just didn't have that vital combination of ingredients that drew it out. **So as a creative exercise, look for that perfect combination constantly.** Ask yourself on a regular basis where it might be, and spend some time really thinking through all this. Creativity takes work; it doesn't just happen by accident. **You get the best ideas by coming up with the *most* ideas; and by asking yourself the best questions, you get the best answers.**

THE MAGIC PILL!

So here's a great question for you. In a perfect world, if you had God-like superpowers and you could offer your prospects and customers anything—and I mean *anything*—what would it be?

Then come up with the most outrageous answers possible, and don't even worry about the consequences. This is a creative exercise, so have fun! Come up with some stupid, wild and crazy things. Later, when you've exhausted yourself, you have time to think, "Well, I can't really do *all* those things, because I don't really have God-like superpowers... **but what can I do that might be similar?**" If you do that consistently enough, your best ideas will get better. This isn't just some fixed little function here; the harder you work at it, the more you'll develop those skills—those mercantile muscles, so to speak.

We have a program right now that's based on watching a couple of our joint venture partners, and noting some of the things they have that are really hot right now. Well, we don't want to just step on their toes and copy exactly what they're doing. They're our friends, right? **However, we can apply some of their good ideas to our own products.** Now, another case we were interested in was something developed by a friend of ours in Florida, whose product required far too much implementation. We didn't want to go through all the headaches and the hassles and the special software development and website technology and all that nonsense—but we did want the basic benefit behind it.

Through the process of discussing all this, Chris Lakey came up with a brilliant idea! It gives our clients the same basic benefit, but we've streamlined it. **We're not stepping on the other guys' toes; we're just giving people something similar,**

and they're loving it! Though it's brand new, already our response rate suggests we might have another Magic Pill on our hands. It's a little too soon to tell, but you never know.

You see, we found something that worked well for other people, then we stripped away some of the negative aspects and the complexities of its implementation, and modified it to avoid plagiarizing the concept—and gave our clients the same basic benefit. Now that we're testing it, we can see exactly how it's working, which is like gangbusters. Now, I told you earlier I didn't like to test... but testing has its good points. When it's all said and done and you put it all together and float it out there, there are moments where you just can't *wait* to wake up and find out how it did that day. So there's some fun to it.

We also have a business within the business that we began about five years ago, at which point we were just raking in the money. I've mentioned this before in the discussion of an earlier principle. This sub-business was bringing in more money than we knew how to intelligently spend—but that was five years ago, and everything changes. Things are slow now; the money is all but dried up, because we've wrung most of the idea's potential out of our list. **We're living in the desert now... but we've found a new way to profit on the idea, and we're in the process of developing that, too.**

Now we're able to give this thing away absolutely free. Well, it's not absolute: there *is* a condition attached, which the customers know upfront. We're not trying to hide it; that's where you run into problems, by initially getting people excited but then making them hate your guts because they find out that there are all kind of catches and gimmicks and tricks and fine print involved. In any case, we're able to give away free what we used to charge for five years ago, when we were rolling in the dough because we were charging for this thing.

Everybody is looking for a Magic Pill—and you have to realize that what that pill is varies according to your business, and who you're serving. The Magic Pill in my marketplace may be different from the magic pill in yours. **Just realize that your prospects are always looking for whatever it is that's going to give them what they want the very most.** That's what you need to look for and respond to, and it all derives from a basic strategy I've talked about over and over again throughout this book: you absolutely have to understand your marketplace at a visceral level.

Such an understanding is much more important than any product or service that you'll ever invent, create, develop or sell. The make-up of your marketplace is the most critical part of the formula, and it's especially true when you talk about finding the Magic Pill. You don't stumble across the Magic Pill by accident; **you have to create it based on what your market most desires—period.** If you create a product or service and *then* go out and try to determine who'll be willing to buy it, you're much less likely to succeed. **Instead, learn who your marketplace is and identify a group of people who are all looking for the same benefits.** *Then* identify the kinds of products and services that those people want the very most.** By starting with the prospect, you can end up creating that Magic Pill product or service.

Now, obviously, if we had the ability, we would *only* create Magic Pills. But there's this huge gap that exists between what we would consider the Magic Pill, and all the stuff we normally sell on a regular basis. We've identified a group of people that we know are interested in the same kinds of things; in our market, the business opportunity market, people who are looking for a way to stay home and make money. **We have a good idea of what they want, and we always attempt to create a Magic Pill service or product for them.** We're always trying to create the next big winner; but you see, what we think doesn't really matter. **It's the marketplace that determines the Magic Pill viability. We only hit that sweet spot every once in a while.**

You have to ask yourself: **if your clients could buy anything they wanted that would provide them any benefit they were after, what would that be? This is what you're trying to get at in your business.** If money was no object, if skill sets and abilities were no object, if they were able to spend whatever it took to buy this item of yours that would provide this benefit... well, what would that be? What would it look like? **That, of course, becomes the Magic Pill.** What the answer is depends on your marketplace. If you serve the diet industry, then the Magic Pill is probably something that makes people lose weight with ease, makes them feel better, makes them fit. If you really had something where all they had to do was sit back and eat whatever they wanted and wake up tomorrow 30 pounds lighter... well, they'd probably pay whatever you're asking, because they really want that benefit, especially if it comes with washboard abs.

In the business opportunity marketplace, most people are looking to either quit their jobs or to supplement their income somehow. Most want to live the entrepreneurial lifestyle, or at least the entrepreneurial lifestyle they perceive—which is basically the lifestyle of not having to work a day in their lives. They want to sit on the beach at the edge of the water, and sip whatever their favorite drink is while watching the sunset. **They want residual income, so that they don't have to actually do anything else to get it.** And if such a thing existed, they would pay whatever price you were asking to receive that benefit. That's the ultimate dream in this marketplace.

Other marketplaces have their own dreams and wishes—things where people are willing to spend whatever amount of money is necessary in order to achieve that result. **Generally speaking, unfortunately, the reason we call it a Magic Pill in the first place is because such a thing doesn't really exist.** In our marketplace, people typically over-simplify what it takes to be successful and have a business that can bring you a lifetime of residual income. They don't really want to put in the time and energy it takes to build such a business, either. People are just as fantasy-prone in the weight-loss industry. Until science comes up with a workable shortcut—and it may—people who want to lose weight will still have to commit to dieting and a rigorous exercise regime no matter what.

A Magic Pill is what you get in a perfect world, when you can create exactly what people want. That's exceedingly rare, but you *can* create the next best thing. **Usually, you can't give people exactly what they want, because it's not practical or it's too expensive.** Sometimes it's physically impossible. You can't really build a time machine, for example. **Therefore, usually there *is* no true Magic Pill—but you want to use that as a reference point, so you can get as close as you can.** That's why you go through testing, through the trial-and-error process. Sometimes things work; sometimes they don't. Occasionally you hit the right combination, the one-two punch that gives you just the right combination of what they're looking for, and your sales and profits will shoot through the roof.

But even that doesn't last forever. Eventually it dies out and you're back to the drawing board, starting the process all over again. **It's a constant game of trying to get inside the heads of your prospects, figuring out what they want the very most, and then trying to find as many ways as possible to give that to them.** And here's something you have to wrap your head around: sometimes what they want the most isn't what you want to give them, or what you think they should want. But that doesn't matter! **You've got to think about what** *they* **want.** Sometimes the dumbest ideas are the ones that work the best, emotionally. It's not always the good thing that drives your customers crazy.

It's all about serving customers, giving them the things they want—as long as you stay within legal boundaries, of course. Do that properly and consistently, and you're likely to eventually find that Magic Pill that results in paydays where the money just comes rolling in effortlessly, because you finally found that right combination. It's like a giant safe where you get all the dials to click just right—and then you can open up the door, and the money just spills out.

✳ ✳ ✳

The adversities in life can make us stronger… and that's great, because business is a constant adversity.

✳ ✳ ✳

Adversity Can Make Us Stronger

The adversities we face in life can make us stronger, and that's a great thing—because business is constant adversity. That's how it seems to me, anyway, and I believe that most other entrepreneurs would say the same.

You know, a lot of people start businesses because they want a better life. The truth is, life (as I know it anyway) is just a constant series of problems, challenges, obstacles, setbacks, disappointments, and suffering at various levels. **And business is life amplified. Now, I'm not saying that life is terrible; it's also full of good stuff, too. You get plenty of that good stuff in business; in fact, generally, you get more of the good than the bad.** But you *do* get plenty of the bad stuff.

While it's true that adversity can break some people, the same adversity can cause other people to break records. There's a quote from Nietzsche that I love: "Whatever doesn't kill you makes you stronger." **In large part, the difficulties we face in life help us develop our skills and abilities, which inevitably makes us stronger.**

In most cases, what matters is what you choose to do with the situation you find yourself in. As another of my favorite quotes points out, **"Adversity introduces you to yourself."** You really find out what you're made of when you have to deal with 10 tons of crap at once. **By taking on more,**

not less, you find out what you're truly capable of. Now, sometimes you do have moments when you break down or have trouble moving forward. **But remember: skills are developed through adversity.** During the smooth times, when everything comes easily, when you're not struggling, when you don't have to pay a large price, you don't really learn anything. You don't develop special abilities and talents.

That's the way most people want to live: they want to move through life unscathed, like they're floating on a gentle, peaceful river. And who can blame them? Who in their right mind *really* wants a life that's filled with all kinds of adversity and challenges? **But when you study the lives of the most successful people, you'll find a common denominator running like a golden thread through their stories: they went through *more* problems than other people, not fewer.** They faced more challenges and struggle than most, and that's part of how they acquired that level of mastery that enabled them to achieve the level of significance that ensures that they actually have a biography that's worth studying.

Again, I'm speaking in generalities here: **but whether you're broken by adversity, or push through it to break records, is based primarily on the way that you look at the problems, obstacles, and setbacks you face.** You can either look at them in a good, positive way, and decide that they're not going to beat you, and keep moving forward—or you can back off.

Back in 1985, when I first decided to go into business for myself, I told a good friend of mine. She was much smarter than me, had much more common sense than I probably still have, and she really cared about me... and so she did everything she could to discourage me. She was unsuccessful, so she went and got another friend of ours, and he started pounding on me too. All their arguments were just so rational: they were just trying to remind me that I had *none* of the qualities that it takes to succeed in business.

And they were right. I *had* none of those qualities then; and 25 years later, in many cases, I still don't. **But I *have* learned to delegate, and I've surrounded myself with people who possess those qualities that I lack. Plus, I was willing to do whatever it took to succeed... and it did require a tremendous price.** I had *no idea* that it was going to take the kind of price that I've had to pay. I'm not complaining or whining; I really don't think that's a bad thing, in any sense. But the fact is that back then, I had absolutely no clue what I was going to have to go through in order to get where I am today... and I probably still have a lot more to go through beyond this. I have no idea, thank God. There's bit of a blessing in being ignorant. I heard, somewhere along the line, that you've got to be a little bit stupid to think you can go out there and make millions of dollars.

I've known a gentleman for 20 years who's a Mensa member—and you have to have an IQ off the charts just to become one. He's got entrepreneurial qualities, and for years I've told him, "Look, you ought to be self−employed. You ought to be an entrepreneur." He's got the desire to do it... but he keeps saying that he knows too many ways that a business can fail. He studied business in college, so he knows about all the things that can go wrong. **Whereas somebody else who lacks that awareness, somebody who's more ignorant than he is, is more likely to charge ahead and plow through it, and just**

figure out a way to make it work.

Skills are developed through adversity—through encountering all the problems and the pain and the setbacks, and trying to make the best of it, trying to salvage some good out of it, trying to turn lemons into lemonade—trying to just not let it defeat you. And it does make you stronger.

Back in 1987, I told my Dad that I was going to get married, and to my face he was supportive. But there are no secrets in my family; everybody loves to gossip. To my sister Carla, my Dad said, "T.J. just isn't ready for marriage." Of course, then she told me, and I got all pissed about it. But you know what? He was right; I *wasn't* ready for marriage. I wasn't ready for business, either. I wasn't ready to take on any of those responsibilities, but the thing is, I would never have been ready for any of it. **There would never have come a perfect time for me to start a business *or* get married—but my marriage and my business are two of the things that give me the greatest satisfaction in life today.** By most people's standards, I would never have been ready; I lacked all of the right qualities, and in some ways I still do—ask my wife! **I still have a long way to go, but I've gotten to where I am by dealing with what I had to deal with and going through it.** That's the way people become strong. That's how they develop.

All of these things have to be developed; that's just reality. But no one likes to talk about adversity. No one likes to admit we're suffering from it. And yet, we all experience it, and it really *can* make you stronger—if we're willing to use it and learn from it. I think the word "can" is important in this principle. **The adversities in life *can* make us stronger; and**

that's great, because business is a constant adversity. I think the opportunity exists for adversity to grow you, if you will; though unfortunately for some people, I think adversity makes them break down. **I think that adversity can wilt a person.** Some people can succumb to it... so ultimately, the opportunity is there for it to have either effect.

How you handle those adversities will determine if it's a growing experience for you. **Martin Luther King, Jr. once said, "The ultimate measure of a man is not where he stands in moments of comfort and convenience, but where he stands at times of challenge and controversy."** So think about that. This could apply to you in any part of your life, business or personally. Your ultimate measure in life or in business is in how you handle and respond to challenges, controversies, inconveniences, and things that don't go your way. It's easy to pretend that life's great when things are going well; it's a lot harder to keep your chin up when you're up against the wall.

When business is going well, money's flowing easily and things are about as good as they could be. Everybody is happy. There are no problems to speak of. In those moments, it's easy to put on a happy face. It's easy to say that everything is going great and that you're doing well, isn't it? Then, when business becomes hard, when things aren't going well, that same person who was so happy when business was good is suddenly crabby to be around. They've always got a frown on their face, or they're always mad. **They're a product of their circumstances, no matter what the circumstances are.** When things are well, they're okay. When things aren't well, they're not so okay.

That's why the measure of a person is more in how they

respond to adversity than how they respond when things are going well. I think that's the point here: **you can be made stronger by adversity, but you have to treat it the right way.** In business, there are always going to be challenges. Even when you have a successful business, there are going to be tough times. Sometimes, successful businesses seem to have big targets on their backs *because* they're successful. **People don't necessarily take to success like you would think they would; some are jealous of it.** If you have a big successful business, your competitors might want to sue you. They might want to talk bad about you in public, or say bad things on the Internet about your company because they don't like you. They think you're too successful. They think you're too big. And of course, if you're big and successful, the government wants a piece of that through a bigger tax percentage, or you may be more prone to get audited by the IRS.

There are all kinds of things that come with success, and then, obviously, on the flip side of that, there are all kinds of problems that occur when things aren't going well and business is suffering. **How you handle those adversities, how you handle the ups and downs, the challenges of business, will determine your ultimate character.** Those things have the opportunities to grow you and make you stronger, but you've got to survive them first. You can't succumb to them.

I'll be the first to admit that business can be frustrating and challenging, especially when you're building a new business. The ultimate success rate for new businesses is about 5%; that is, approximately 95% of businesses don't make it to their fifth anniversary. Even among the 5% that do, some just barely make it. Many of those businesses face a ton of things that don't go right during that initial start-up and growth phase. **Well, the ability of those business owners to see it through those times when things are ugly has a lot to do with whether they make it to that five year mark or not.** When things aren't going well, you really do learn a lot more about your mettle, and your ability and desire to stick it out.

Adversities can make you stronger, if you'll let them — and if you'll work through them and use them as a springboard to future success. So adversity isn't a foreign concept; we all deal with it. **How you respond to it will determine, ultimately, your success or failure.** If you study the biographies of successful people, you'll see a pattern of them going through some very difficult periods; and yet they got through it all, and in the end things worked out for them. The same thing can happen to you, too.

And just as adversity introduces you to yourself, it also introduces you to the people around you. **The best way to find out about other people, and to find out what they're made of, is go through some difficulty with them.**

CHAPTER THREE

MOST self-employed people have a terrible boss!

Most Self-Employed People Have a Terrible Boss!

Most self-employed people have a terrible boss. **That statement sound a little cute, but it's also *true*.** They say that if you get into legal trouble, the worst thing you can do is try to represent yourself in a court of law; you would be your own worst lawyer. It's the same thing with business.

Let's go back to that friend of mine I was talking about, **the one who isn't committed enough to really succeed.** He's been self-employed for a good number of years now. He has a business, but he's interested in so many different things, and there are so many chances for him to screw around and do everything *except* anything that has to do with his business. **That's one of the reasons why he's always struggled financially: there are so many distractions.** Now, no boss would ever let anybody screw around the way a lot of entrepreneurs allow themselves to. **So just as you wouldn't want to be your own lawyer, you really don't want to be your own boss. On the other hand, it's unavoidable as an entrepreneur!**

Here are a few ways to overcome that problem. First of all, you have to know your strengths and be honest about your weaknesses. I've talked about this before. **You can't fail to take your weaknesses into account;** you've got to take a long, hard look at the things you're not good at, be honest about them, and then delegate them to others who can do them better. **Build a team; find other people who are strong in the areas you're weak in.** A company is a combination of different people working together. **You've got to build that team, and then set your goals very high.** By experimenting with dozens of ideas, you can find those few things that you can mix up a little to achieve your own highest level of productivity. There are all kinds of things you can experiment with.

Here's an example of one of the things I do in order to be very productive. As I write, I'm six days into a lead fulfillment project. I've got one good day left, and I think I can get it done. So I'll have seven days into it, total. Well, during these last six days, I have just worked my butt off. **One of the reasons I've worked my butt off is because the initial lead generation package is on the press and, if not this week, it'll be dropping the first of next week.** I've got to get this fulfillment package done. If there's one thing I can't stand more than any other, it's to have leads growing cold, because you don't have anything to send to them. It just drives me crazy.

This is just an idea, just something we do within our business. But we'll go ahead and throw the lead generation pieces out there, as I've done now on this piece. **And then, because it drives us crazy to have leads sitting around, we'll work harder.** We'll burn the midnight oil. We'll put in lots and lots of concentrated, focused, intense work of the kind that's unimaginable to most people, because we set it up that way to begin with.

These are things that you do consciously. **Experiment; be creative.** This is just one example of what we do within our

36

business, but there are plenty of things that you can do—and you're only going to find them by experimenting with a lot of things. **Find the things that cause you to work at your highest level, things that force you to be your most productive.** By trying dozens of different things, you'll find a handful that work very well for you. You'll end up working, in some ways, like my example, where we throw these lead generation pieces out there before we have the actual fulfillment materials complete.

It's a way of boxing ourselves in a corner and committing. It's a leap of faith. It's a real commitment. **What you're doing is creating a problem, and then solving that problem.** You're saying, "Bring it on; I can handle that." Without having any real idea about exactly how we're going to put these things together, we make lots of promises to our customers, knowing *vaguely* how we're going to put it all together, knowing that we *can* put it all together... and then we just scramble like hell to figure it out.

What we do then is force ourselves to do what every good boss wants you to do, which is to work your fanny off. Is there any boss who *doesn't* want you to work as hard as you can? When you're your own boss, you've got to do things that keep the blinders on, so to speak, and **give yourself a little taste of the whip every now and then to get yourself moving, to help you stay focused.**

Now, I'll also say that there is power in leverage, and as a leverage principle, a lot of entrepreneurs are actually just high-paid employees themselves. What they should be doing is working *on* the business, rather than working in it. That means different things to different businesses, of course; but essentially,

working on the business is where you're tightly focused on the two areas of the business that actually produce a profit, which are marketing and innovation. Marketing, again, is the acquisition and retention of customers; innovation is all those things that make people in the market salivate and want to keep coming back and doing more business with you. If you're totally focused on those areas of the business, then you're working at a higher level than someone who stuffs envelopes. Anybody can do low-level minimum wage work; you don't want to waste your time doing that.

The point is, you want to handle the things that require a higher degree of skill, ability, and talent, rather than just doing the necessary work. It's good, valuable work, but it's the kind of work that almost anybody can do. **As the entrepreneur and business owner, you want to focus on things that only you can do, and that you can do best.** Last, but not least, you don't want to burn out. **So you've got to pace yourself; but you also have to *push* yourself, and learn how to be the most productive worker you can be.**

This whole concept involves realizing, in a visceral way, that as a self-employed individual, you're not the best possible boss. There are a lot of people who really just need to work for other people. Those who are poor time managers, who aren't good self-starters, or who can't manage themselves well in general *need* to work for somebody else, because they need someone to tell them when to work and when to take a break, and when to go home. They don't do very good at keeping themselves busy, doing the things in their businesses that need to be done. If you're like that, and your boss can't keep you in line, then they're not doing a good job as a boss. It's even worse when you're self-employed, so that *you* are the boss.

If you're deep in the trenches in your business, and you have problems keeping yourself in line, then you absolutely have to find a way to be a better boss, to manage yourself better than you do already. **Mostly that comes down to self-discipline. The way to get better at something is to become more committed to it.**

Chris Lakey has a bass guitar that he bought because he always thought it would be fun just to play around with. He wasn't sure whether he'd be committed to learning it or not, he tells me, and it turns out that he really doesn't have the time to learn to play it... or at least, he hasn't *taken* the time to learn. **He has just as much time as everybody else does, but he chooses to do different things with it.** So clearly, Chris isn't a very good boss when it comes to teaching himself how to play bass guitar, even though he has one and he's fully capable of learning. A musician is never going to be able to master an instrument unless they're committed to the time it takes to learn the basics and then practice, practice, practice.

For an athlete, it's the same way. **An athlete's performance is never going to improve unless they practice.** They have to be committed to being better at whatever their sport is. If they're a football player, they've got to commit to better conditioning so they can play more. They've got to be faster, stronger. A basketball player has to be committed to trying to make more shots. A lot of basketball players struggle at the free throw line, so clearly, they've got to get better at shooting free throws. These are the things a coach can stay on them about. **But to a large degree, it's up to them to be responsible for their own actions and to be committed to improving in these areas.**

In the same way, entrepreneurs (or any self-employed people) have to become better at pushing themselves. They've got to find ways to do things that make them more productive, so they can get the job done faster and more efficiently. The strategies that you put in place to do that will determine how good you are at being a boss for yourself. **I think being a good self-boss, if you will, is mostly about using willpower and self-discipline to drive you towards the ends that you're trying to achieve, and setting specific actions in place to become a better manager of your own time and the processes that you employ every day in your attempt to be successful.**

Most self-employed people aren't very good at that, and the ones that succeed the best are the ones who can find a way to pull out the best in themselves. **And you *can* develop the abilities necessary to do that.** As the old saying goes, where there's a will, there's a way. **Your best can continue to get better, as long as you continue pushing forward, keep learning to handle yourself and your time more efficiently, and above all, never stop fighting to overcome all those challenges in your way.**

CHAPTER FOUR

The 4 laws of self teaching:

1. *You are your greatest teacher.*

2. You can learn <u>anything</u> you want to learn.

3. You <u>must</u> take total responsibility for everything that happens to you.

4. Experience + Reflection = Wisdom!

The Four Laws of Self-Teaching

Let's move on to a few Ways that are rather philosophical in nature. The first one is something called "The Four Laws of Self-Teaching." I got this out of a book years back, and it made so much sense to me that I wrote it down and I've followed it ever since.

My friend Allen once gave me a "No Gurus" button: that is, it said, "Gurus" on it, with an X through it. I understood the concept instantly. You see, there are just so many people looking for answers when it comes to making money. They're looking for other people to point them in the right direction; there's no question about that. And I do think that finding people who can help you in that way is very important; but ultimately, you've got to figure things out for yourself. **Others can point the way, but you have to develop your own understanding of a particular subject. That's the FIRST law of self-teaching:** *You are your own greatest teacher. Think things through for yourself.*

The SECOND law is: *You can learn anything that you* <u>*want*</u> *to learn.* The keyword here is *want*. It's your desire to learn something that makes all the difference. **The more you want something, the less work it's going to be to achieve it, and the more willing you're going to be to pay the price to get there.** There's always a learning curve, and you have to go into the project willing to pay the necessary price. Sadly, a lot of people want the result. but don't necessarily want to put in the time and the effort required to go through that learning curve, which is always painful. But let's get real: **when you truly want something, you've *got* to be willing to pay a price for it.** That price probably isn't going to feel good; sorry. But the more you want it, the easier it is to pay the price. You've probably seen this in your own life.

My best example is public speaking. I've always admired public speakers. I've always loved a good preacher or politician—those natural salespeople who can get up in front of an audience and say whatever they want with a minimum of difficulty. Yet speaking in front of a group just absolutely terrified me when I first got started in this business... **yet I wanted to do it so badly that I was willing to go through 10 years of absolute hell to learn how.** It's still not always easy for me, but I'm through the worst of it. For 10 years, though, it was hell on Earth. It was terrible getting sick before a speech, throwing up in the bathroom before I went on, losing my voice, sweating profusely, or screwing up in front of a crowd (which I still do occasionally), all simply because fear petrified me. But I wanted to do it so bad that it made paying that price a lot easier.

I can say the same thing about several other skills that I've developed. Not that I'm a master at any of these skills, but I'm constantly getting closer to being the best I can possibly be. **You really *can* teach yourself anything that you want to— assuming you want to learn it badly enough.**

The THIRD law, I believe, is the most important: *You must assume total responsibility for everything that happens to you. Everything.* I know that people sometimes get into situations beyond their control; and they say, "Well, do I have to take responsibility for that?" No, not as such. **You must, however, take responsibility for your reaction to the situation (or your lack of reaction) at the very least.** The opposite of being responsible is being a victim, and the weakest people on Earth are victims. Victims are always blaming other people, events, or situations for their misfortune. That's what children do, by the way. Kids always want to blame; and that's a sign of immaturity that we're all supposed to outgrow. Yet I see so many adults still running around playing the blame game. They're still victims. They're blaming other people and random events for everything. It's not their fault. They're pissed off at the world, they're bitter, they're cynical, and it's always *somebody else's fault*.

Unless and until you assume full responsibility for your actions and your reactions to things that you can't control, you're never going to reach your full potential. Back in the 1930s, a very successful business woman named Mary Parker Follett pointed out, **"Responsibility is the great developer of men."** She was talking about mankind here, by the way, not males in particularly. Sometimes, whenever things get really stressful, I'll quote that to myself over and over again. When I feel like I'm taking on the weight of the whole world and can't assume any more responsibility, I'll say to myself, "Responsibility is the great developer of men." **Assuming responsibility for yourself is the opposite of weakness. It's the price you pay for success. It's a strength.**

The FOURTH law is this: *Wisdom must be developed.* **Basically, experience plus reflection equals wisdom.** You've got to make a lot of mistakes along the way; that's where you get the experience. I wish there was a better way, but there really isn't. Sometimes, if you're really smart, you can learn from the mistakes of others; but again, remember the first law: *You are your greatest teacher.* **So get ready to make a lot of mistakes and learn from them; that's where you get experience.** Then you reflect on all that, you think things through, and ultimately you do develop wisdom. And it does have to be developed, because it doesn't always come naturally, and it's definitely something that you can't just get out of a book.

You've got to learn things for yourself, so you've got to make a lot of mistakes. **Try making new mistakes when you do; don't just keep repeating the same dumb mistakes over and over again.** Learn something. Teach yourself. Assume total responsibility so that when you make mistakes, you don't blame somebody else, and you just keep learning.

I realize that this entire concept of self-teaching seems alien to most modern Americans; and I think that's probably because most of us need to change the way we think about education. While I don't want to go into all of my concerns about education in the United States today, I do want you to think about how we educate people; because I think it's important to remember what options you have out there. I'm not talking about anything specific, but in a general sense. Just think about education today. We tend to be spoon-fed knowledge—and then only the things that the system thinks we need to know to get by.

The way it works for most of us is that at a very young age, you enter into a school program of some kind. Many children start preschool at age three or four. As he or she grows up, a kid will go through kindergarten and elementary school before moving on to some sort of middle school or junior high; it's called different things in different places, though some places have both middle schools *and* junior highs. Then they move into high school. After they graduate, most people continue their education in some sort of college program. **After they graduate that (or not, as the case may be) they enter the workforce— and education stops for most people.** That's basically what people think of when they think "education": a formal situation where someone is instructed on how to think by some kind of teacher or professor, and then given measured amounts of whatever that teacher or professor thinks they need to know. That's what education looks like in the United States these days.

Self-teaching is a completely different type of education, and I suspect it may be more productive and useful than formal education in the long run. It's possible that most people would be better off being self-taught past high school, in fact, rather than going to university and racking up high levels of debt to acquire degrees that often don't help them accomplish much. **Being self-taught has a lot of advantages;** and you know, here's the funny thing. Historically, if you look back at our country's founding, you'll see that a lot of the Founding Fathers were self-taught. Not all of them attended fancy colleges; Patrick Henry, for example, was a self-taught lawyer. Now, think about that. How likely is that today? Not very. I'd say the possibility is nil, zip, naught. It doesn't happen now— the legal profession wouldn't allow it—but it did a couple of hundred years ago.

From a philosophical point, there's no reason you shouldn't

be self-taught. I believe that assuming that you *must* have a formalized education in order to succeed in the world reveals a flaw in your thinking. **You really are your greatest teacher; think about all the things that you've been interested in, the things that you wanted to discover or learn on your own, and then contrast that with when you were in school.** When I was in school, I was a slacker. It wasn't that I really was necessarily uninterested in knowledge; I just wasn't a very good student and didn't really care much about what I was learning. Since then, I've developed a hunger for knowledge on a few specific subjects, which I focus on and develop my own education in.

I know that Chris Lakey is the same way. He's a technological junkie, so he likes reading about things that are tech-related. He's also a political junkie, so he likes learning about politics and political issues. He likes reading about our Founders and the way our country is supposed to be run and governed, based on their original precepts. Chris soaks up those things like a sponge, because he's very interested in those subjects. **You *always* learn better when you're interested in the things you're learning about.**

And in our society, you can learn just about anything you want to. **I think it's important to remember that the requisite knowledge is out there for anybody who wants to go after it, especially since the Internet exploded on the scene.** It doesn't seem to matter what your socioeconomic status is. Lots of poor people have plenty of knowledge; just because they might not have a job, or might have a crappy job, doesn't mean they're dumb. A homeless person can be just as intelligent as a Harvard graduate. You may question that notion, but it's true. **Just**

because someone's poor at any moment, or just because someone might be homeless, doesn't mean that they don't have knowledge.

Most people have the ability to learn anything that they want to learn about anything. Hey, it's free to go to the library. Whether you're poor or homeless, whether you're a new college graduate or have a Fortune 500 job, the library is full of all kinds of books on all kinds of things. Almost all libraries have Web connectivity, too. **A hunger for knowledge leads people to learn whatever it is they want to learn.** You can become an expert on anything you want to become an expert on, *if* you're determined to become knowledgeable at it. This assumes, of course, that you do take total responsibility for everything that happens to you. When it comes to self-teaching, the buck stops with you. **If you want to learn something, only you can determine whether you *will* learn it.** Only you can determine whether you will succeed in it, whatever it is. If you lack the willpower to educate yourself, you can't justifiably fault anybody else. If you want to know it, go out and learn it. If you want to just discover something, go discover it. *You have to take responsibility for your own education.*

Finally, let me re-emphasize that experience plus reflection equals wisdom. **The more you discover, the more you *want* to discover.** Chris tells me that he's found this to be true with politics, with his quest for knowledge about where we came from as a country, and where we went wrong (in his opinion), and some of the things that he thinks need to happen for us to fix the problems we find ourselves in as a nation. The more you learn on any subject, the more you experience, the more you think about it—that's where the wisdom comes from. **Then you use that as a launching pad for gaining more knowledge and more wisdom.** It just continues to grow and snowball as discovery takes place, and as you become more and more self-taught.

Again, consider Patrick Henry, who was a self-taught attorney. Eventually, he had enough knowledge to feel that he could practice law. I'm sure there was some point when he said to himself, "I know a little, but I don't know enough to feel like I can be an attorney." At some point, though, he became knowledgeable enough to actually put his education and self-teaching into practice. You can do the same. **Whatever you want to learn, you simply have to be determined to do it, to take responsibility first for your own actions and your learning, and then your determination to succeed at it. And don't give up!** Be willing to stick to it. Because it *will* be hard, especially when you're learning a new skill or a subject. Be determined, be willing to do whatever it takes, and you can be self-taught in whatever it is that you want, whatever you have a hunger of knowledge for.

CHAPTER FIVE

Step out in faith — and figure it out *as you go!*

Step Out In Faith

Step out in faith, and figure it out as you go: that's one secret to success, and it *is* a secret, if only because so many people refuse to accept the concept as valid! So many folks want to have everything figured out in advance. They want to map it all out and be prepared for whatever may come. So they try to think everything through... and then they get paralyzed because they can't even get started. Even if they do get moving, they're soon hit with the reality that our plans never work out the way we want them to. As the saying goes, no battle plan ever survives contact with the enemy.

A better strategy is to set the goal and commit to a direction, mapping out some very loose strategy in the beginning before moving forward. You try a lot of things, you make a lot of mistakes, and you just figure things out as you go. This is commonly referred to as the **"Ready, Fire, Aim" method,** because everybody's heard the opposite: "Ready, Aim, Fire." Just figure it out as you move forward, crossing the bridges as you come to them. **Now, it takes great courage to do this, and that's why so many people just don't.** They're afraid; and because they're afraid, they hold back, and want to sit there and overanalyze everything, making sure every little thing is perfect before they make a move. **This level of perfectionism can defeat you.**

I'll be the first to admit that, to a certain level, you often *do* have to have things figured out before you make your move. **You can't jump into most situations completely blind and expect to come up smelling like a rose.** Just don't take your advance preparation to a ridiculous extent! Here at M.O.R.E., Inc., we're getting ready to move into a whole new direction with our business, and we're ready to run some lead generation ads. We're moving into a market that we don't have a whole lot of experience with. So before we run our lead generation ads, we want to make sure our initial lead fulfillment is all ready to go. That's about as prepared as we get. Otherwise, we've got four very loose plans that we're going to test, so we can find out what works best.

Again, you figure it out as you go along. **You try different things, do more of whatever works, and do less of whatever doesn't; it's as simple as that.** When it comes to making money, you can sit there and try to figure it out forever... but no matter what, as soon as you step out in faith, you're going to get blindsided. All of a sudden, your plans are going to be pretty much worthless. The real world has a way of doing that. **Your best approach is to screw up your courage, pick a general direction, set some goals, get moving, and just learn as you go.** Be willing to do whatever it takes to make it.

The late, great Gary Halbert use to say, **"You can learn more through movement than meditation."** This ties directly in with the last Way that we talked about: the Four Laws of Self-Teaching. Now, a little reflection is necessary to develop wisdom; but if you just sit on your rear end and try to reflect all the time, you're never going to get anywhere. The only way you can get anywhere is to go out there and try a lot of different things, to be willing to do whatever it takes, to commit yourself to a certain direction, and to try to learn as you go along. **You have to fight your tendency to have it all figured out before you set out.**

Most of us have at least one subject we're fanatical about preparing for. Chris Lakey says he's this way about travel. He has to have every detail plotted out in advance. He can't even leave the house on vacation without having pulled up at least three different maps to figure out where he's going, usually online or, these days, on his phone. He's usually got a map on his phone that he charts it out on, even after printing a map from Google so he has a hard copy. He makes sure all his hotels are confirmed and double-checked. He gets everything all situated before he leaves, because he wants to make sure he knows exactly where he's going. He wants to make sure he knows how long it's supposed to take. He wants to make sure he knows how many stops he needs to make. **He has to have it all charted out before he steps foot out the door.**

Chris even frets when he's in the car, even before he leaves the driveway; he's thinking, *Did I miss anything? Did I forget something? Is there some detail that I needed to go back over again?* In general, Chris is just very detail-oriented when he travels—and people are that way in a lot of different things. Some people are that way in business, where they feel they always have to have every last detail figured out. **But I honestly think that when it comes to business, when it comes to making money, you have to be more flexible than that.** It may be that you're trying to learn how to do something new, and you're entering a new marketplace or a new area—some kind of fresh, challenging venture. **The temptation is to get every "i" dotted, every "t" crossed.** The temptation is to know everything there is to know.

Unfortunately, that's rarely possible. **In many cases, that leads to inaction. You're waiting for everything to be perfect, and that never happens. So you're paralyzed and you never actually get out there and start making money.** Instead of allowing yourself to be paralyzed, you've *got* to step out in faith and be willing to figure it out as you go. You'll make mistakes, and it won't always be easy; in fact, sometimes it's very challenging *because* you don't have it all figured out. **But compare stepping out on faith and a dream and a hope, and having some challenges but getting somewhere, versus sitting on home plate and waiting for the ball to come. It never happens; you just keep sitting there.** When you wait for the perfect scenario, when you wait for "everything to be figured out," you lock yourself into inaction and get bogged down. Just go. **Just do something, even if you end up making a few mistakes.**

As an analogy, there are two strategies to playing golf. One would be to try to learn everything you can and master the game beforehand, and then go play your first 18 holes months later. The second would be just to grab some clubs and start hacking away. Given a long enough time, both methods will produce a golfer, and you'll definitely be golfing eventually. But in the second scenario, you'll be golfing a lot faster. **If you just get out there and start playing the game, you're going to learn and get better as you go. That's a natural process.**

It's the same way in business. You may struggle a bit in the process. You may have some things that don't go quite as well as you may like—but you're out there doing it. You're having fun. You're living the dream. You've got your own thing going, whatever that thing is. You're living that entrepreneurial lifestyle. **You're making adjustments as you go, and you're figuring it all out.** Hopefully you're not losing too much money in the beginning, although a lot of businesses do lose money as they struggle to get started. **There's an undeniable learning curve,** and in some businesses, it can take you a few years to turn a profit once you get started. It all depends on your business model, and precisely what you're doing to bring it about.

But getting out there and just going is the key, because if you stop and wait for the perfect opportunity, you won't ever get one. Perfection is the realm of the divine; it never happens here on Earth. You can't sit there in the starting gate waiting for the perfect time, because that's never going to come. **An object in motion tends to stay in motion... and unfortunately, an object sitting still tends to stay sitting still. So get out there. Step out in faith and figure it out as you go.**

CHAPTER SIX

The great Olympic runner,
Steve Prefontaine said:

"There may be men who can beat me — but they'll have to bleed to do it!"

Be a Fighter

The late long-distance runner Steve Prefontaine, who was a truly remarkable athlete, once said about running, **"There may be men who can beat me, but they'll have to bleed to do it."**

When I first heard that line, I thought of the greatest entrepreneurs I knew of, because of all the many things they have in common, first and foremost, **they're** *fighters*. **They've got that competitive spirit.** You can knock them down a thousand times and they'll get up a thousand and one times. They refuse to be stopped. There's nothing that can stop these people. They're like the "Terminators" of business. They just keep moving forward, no matter what you throw in their face. Oh, you can slow them down; you can even knock them down. **You can beat the crap out of them, but they won't break. They just keep going and going until finally they succeed or die.** They're the competitors who refuse to quit.

One of my very favorite movies, which I try to watch once every couple of years, was made in 1967. The movie is *Cool Hand Luke,* with Paul Newman and George Kennedy. There's a scene in that movie where George Kennedy and Paul Newman are fighting in a ring. So here's Paul, of average build, kind of a wiry, thin guy. And here's George, this big NFL linebacker type of guy, and George is just beating the crap out of Paul, knocking him to the ground repeatedly, just beating him bloody. And Paul

THE MAGIC PILL!

Newman's character keeps getting up, keeps brushing the dust off of himself, and keeps trying to fight—even though he can't fight. He's so weak he's pretty close to death—but he refuses to quit. **He refuses to be beaten.** No matter how many times he gets knocked down, he just keeps getting back up. People around him are saying, "Stay down, stay down, stay down," but he won't stay down. Finally, George Kennedy's character has two choices. He can either kill Luke, which is going to happen if he keeps it up, or he can concede. That's what he does. Ultimately, Luke wins the fight because he just refuses to quit.

This idea that there's such a thing as failure—I wish you'd get that idea out of your head. *There is no such thing as failure.* Well, wait a minute... yeah, there is. What am I saying? Of course there's such a thing as failure. **Failure is when you finally just give up. Other than that, as long as you're not quitting, as long as you're continuing to move forward, you can't fail.** You may go through some really hard times, and it may feel like you're failing. In the short term you may not achieve the results you want—but that's not the same thing as failure. So keep fighting.

I've got a Theodore Roosevelt quote up on my wall that I look at all the time: "Unreasonable people rule the world." You see, people who are "reasonable" look too hard at the risks involved in a new project and decide, "Oh, man, I can't do that. Too risky." Everything has to be perfect before they begin, so they try to think everything through first; and the first time things really go wrong and everything gets all screwed up, these reasonable people quit. They're not going to pay a large price for anything. **They're just going to try to skate through life as**

unscathed as they possibly can, tiptoeing along until they make it to death.

But entrepreneurs are very unreasonable people. They're always going out there and trying all kinds of unreasonable things. They're willing to pay a tremendous price to get what they want. They have huge goals and dreams. The reasonable people are looking at them and scratching their heads, thinking they're a little crazy. That's just the way it is. They're willing to pay the price. **They're willing to sacrifice, and they're willing to go through a lot of pain and suffering to achieve success.**

There was a time when my business was so bad, it looked like I was going to have to declare bankruptcy. I didn't think I had any other choice. I'd made a number of mistakes that brought me to that point, and I was facing a few things that were beyond my control; but still, **the buck stops with me.** But I *didn't* have to declare bankruptcy, thanks to the fact that I got a lot of help from my staff—all credit where it's due. **I've surrounded myself with a good team of people. Nothing can replace that, and the fact that we all refused to quit.** We pulled out of it. We made it through it.

During this time, I was being audited by the IRS. I had to go speak to this IRS agent several times, and she knew how bad business was. It was all right there in the numbers; we were barely making it. And yet, she suspected me of wrongdoing somehow. Even though she never accused me directly, I finally figured out what the real issue was. After we skated around the subject for a while, I just asked flat out, "You think that I've been hiding money or taking money from the company somehow, don't you?"

She never said, "Yes, I do think that." What she said was, "I just don't see why, if your business is this bad, you're continuing to move forward." I told her, "Look. If I was a more reasonable person, I would have declared bankruptcy. I would have given up. **But I care about this business. I love it; I'm passionate about it. This is my life. And I'm not going to quit. I'm going to continue to fight as long as I can.**" The more I think about this, the more years that have gone by since I dealt with the situation, the more I believe that, as an employee of the government, she expects people to quit and move on to another job when the going gets tough.

Entrepreneurs aren't like that. We're in it to win it. Nothing can stop us; we're going to fight to our last breaths. We're the warriors of the business world: no question about it. I hope you'll take this attitude to heart: this Steve Prefontaine attitude of "There may be men who can beat me, but they'll have to bleed to do it." **That quote represents the ultimate competitive spirit, and it invests you with an energy that keeps you moving forward with such vigor that you can't be easily stopped.** It's a challenge to the world; you're saying, **"Hey, you want to beat me? You're going to have to get dirty. It's going to get ugly. There's going to be blood involved."** Now, I've seen enough track events to know that sometimes, they do get really bloodied and banged up. I've seen these horrible crashes on the track—they miss a hurdle, or their foot kicks it, or they get bumped, and they go down on their knees hard. A runner who falls down like that can get really bloodied up. They might take a big chunk out of their knee and scrape their elbows.

It's much the same in business. One of the core business-building strategies that we teach here at M.O.R.E., Inc. is the concept of **ruthless marketing. It's an honest but no-holds-barred attitude toward beating your competition.** So think about your own business; and realize that if you're doing the absolute best you can at marketing your business, if you're doing everything you can to be aggressive in your marketplace and to be as successful as you can be, then you'll be able to use this quote by Steve Prefontaine. Insert the name of your business or the industry that you're in: "There may be carpet cleaners, or chiropractors, or restaurants in this town that can beat me, but they'll have to bleed to do it."

When you decide to personalize this concept to your business, start by thinking about how you want to be known in your industry by your competitors, not necessarily by your customers. **You want to be that aggressive business in your marketplace that people aspire to beat.** You want to be able to shout from the rooftops, "If you want to beat me at my game, you may be able to do it—but it's going to cost you dearly! It's going to cost you in blood, sweat, and tears! If you want to beat me, you're going to have to be willing to accept the battle wounds to *prove* that you've beaten me!"

When you think about winning, when you think about competition and about coming out the victor, understand that the victor usually isn't the one who tried the least, or who put the least amount of energy into the effort. He's not the one who moped along and lollygagged around. **The businesses that succeed usually aren't the ones that are passive.** They're not the ones who just wish and hope that people will find their doorstep and come on in, and think, "Golly gee, wouldn't it be nice if people bought something from me every once in a while?" That's *not* who you think of when you think of winning businesses. You think of the businesses that out there are pounding the pavement, hustling, doing what it takes to succeed and win in their marketplace. If you want to have that kind of business, then you've got to be up on your game. **Your game has to be at its maximum.** You have to be like Steve Prefontaine, or that $20-million-a-picture actor.

From that perch, from you sitting on top in that position of power in your market, you can look down on your competition as they sit below you in the marketplace —not in a demeaning way, but from a position of power, so that you can say to them, "I'm the king of the hill. If you want to beat me, if you want to knock me off of my perch, you're going to have to invest some blood, some sweat, and some tears. You're going to have to try harder." **They may very well step up to the challenge. You may not be able to stay on top; but at least you'll know you did everything you could do to stay there.**

You don't win them all. If you know'you tried your hardest and you've put your guts into it and didn't come out on top, at least you can say you laid it all on the line and that there was nothing left on the table. **You had nothing more in you.** It's kind of like a runner who gives it all over the first three-quarters of the race; and then, as they cross the finish line, they literally collapse, because they *have* put it all on the line. As they cross the goal and win the prize, there's nothing left in the tank. They have nothing more to give. They've finished the race using every last bit of effort and energy.

That's what it's like to put it all out there. You can do that in business; and then when you do, you're in the position to be able to tell people that if they want to beat you, they're going to have to bleed.

CHAPTER SEVEN

Product knowledge is highly overrated.

Every salesperson is trained in extensive product knowledge. <u>FORGET</u> <u>THAT</u>! <u>Prospect</u> <u>knowledge</u> <u>is</u> <u>more</u> <u>important</u> <u>than</u> <u>product</u> <u>knowledge</u>. Prospects buy perceived benefits and results. They do not buy product information.

Develop Your
Prospect Knowledge First

Every salesperson is trained in extensive product knowledge. Forget that! ***Prospect* knowledge is more important than product knowledge. Always. Prospects buy perceived benefits and results;** they don't buy products for the sake of buying products. Think about that. **The market comes first; the product evolves from and revolves around the people in your marketplace. It starts and ends with them.**

So sit down and ask yourself the questions: who are the best prospective buyers in my market? What are they really looking for? What do they want more than anything else? Why are they buying the kinds of products that my competitors are selling, or the kinds of items that I've sold in the past? If you've been in business for a while, ask yourself, What are my best-selling items? What do people want more of? What aren't they getting?

We use something called the "perfect world scenario" when we're brainstorming ideas. **Ask yourself: In a perfect world, if I had godlike superpowers and could come up with exactly what people wanted to buy, what would that be?** Then you brainstorm with all kinds of crazy answers—even ones that seem impossible to provide at first glance. The ideas may seem crazy, but those crazy answers often lead to the truth.

In our particular market, right or wrong, good or bad, what

people really want is an investment. Well, we don't sell investments; we're not licensed to do so. We sell business opportunities. **But still, what the people in the opportunity market** *really* **want is an investment opportunity, because the flat truth of the matter is that the large majority of the people in this marketplace at this particular time want somebody else to do it all for them.** I'm not being judgmental here, just recognizing the reality of the situation. If we really did live in a perfect world, and if we had godlike superpowers, we could give them precisely what they want. We'd give them an investment where they could put in $1,000, and then let us take care of everything—and they could more than double that money in a short time. And so, **we try to develop business opportunities that provide those benefits,** even though we absolutely, positively don't sell investments or securities or anything of that nature.

Remember: the prospects always come first. **What do they really, really want?**

You need to try to give exactly that to them, even if, on the face of it, it doesn't seem realistic. I'm not saying that you should lie; just be very cognizant of this fact, and be sure that you can offer your prospects what they want in a way that they can accept. Back in 1997, we had our very first $5,000 seminar. We were really scared, too: we'd never sold a seminar on our own for that much. So we were upstairs planning things out before the seminar and somebody said, "Look, let's not talk about all this 'get rich quick' stuff. Let's tell people that the first year, they can make $50,000 a year. The next year, they can double that. The next year they can double *that*—and ultimately they can make millions of dollars over a longer period of time."

We all decided, "You know what? That's the way to go. Let's just be real. Let's be reasonable with these people." So we went downstairs and opened up the seminar, with over 100 people in the audience. They've all paid $5,000 to be there; and I got up on stage and asked, "Okay! Who here wants to make $50,000 in your first year?" Well, you could have heard a pin drop. The vibes were just so thick; people were like the deer in the headlights. They were just totally freaked out. After a few seconds of very uncomfortable silence, I came to my senses and asked enthusiastically, "Who here wants to make millions of dollars?" And everybody just jumped up and started shouting.

That's how we began the seminar. It was party time! **They all wanted to make millions of dollars, and the truth was, they *could* do so.** They simply didn't want to start slowly. They didn't care to go from $50,000 to $100,000, to $250,000, to $500,000, and then make millions of dollars in their fifth year or tenth year. They didn't want to do anything like that. They wanted to make millions of dollars *now*. That's a fundamental personality aspect of the people in our marketplace. **They're enthusiastic about making lots of money right away, so we have to cater to what they want.**

The same is true in any marketplace. **You have to know the market intimately.** What do they want more than anything else in the world? How can you give it to them, and serve it up better and bigger than any of your other competitors... and stay out of legal trouble in the process? **Until you know that, you can't worry about a particular product**! People tend to forget this—even experienced entrepreneurs who should know better.

73

THE MAGIC PILL!

They think, "Well, if I want to sell this product to people, I should know everything there is to know about it. That knowledge of the product will help me sell it to a customer." That's true, and it's important, but *not* until you're an expert on the customers you're selling to. **People tend to forget about the customer, sadly.**

In a former life, Chris Lakey sold cars for a short while. One of the things they taught him was not to be so focused on a car's features as opposed to the overall benefits of the vehicle for the prospect who was thinking about buying it. For example, if he had a mom on the lot who had her two kids with her and she was looking at a minivan, he didn't need to talk about how much horsepower was under the hood. Now, that doesn't mean that every mom doesn't know or care about horsepower, but by and large mothers are more concerned about whether the minivan has airbags and if it has a DVD player in the back. On the flipside, if he had a young business guy in, and the prospect was looking at a sports car, of course Chris would talk about how fast the car was, and how slick it looked going down the street, and how the prospect could imagine himself cruising through town with the top down and his hair blowing in the wind, and how hot he would look to all the ladies.

Chris would talk about the benefits that were important to that particular prospect. He had to do quite a bit of thinking on his feet, because the prospects who come onto a car lot are really varied. He had all kinds of people who were concerned about all kinds of things; there were many reasons why they might be interested in a particular vehicle.

In any marketplace, you start with the knowledge of

who you're selling to, and then you pitch to them based on whatever's most important to them. Those things come out in the benefits that are delivered when they do business with you, not so much in the features of a particular product. Again, in selling cars, Chris talked less about the specific features of a vehicle and more about what those features would do for someone. While you do need to have up-to-date product knowledge, that knowledge truly is overrated; **it's much more important for you to learn who your customer is, and what they want or need, and how you can offer them a solution.** I don't think that there's a better foundational principle for sales than this one.

This does require some flexibility, and as I've mentioned, you have to stay on your toes in order to maximize your sales potential. Let's say you do phone sales. It doesn't really matter what you sell: what matters is that when you're talking to someone, trying to make that sale, you're paying attention to what they're telling you they want. **You know _in general_ what your marketplace wants, but in each case you're following their cues to figure out the things that are important to them specifically.** You're using that knowledge to present your product or service as a solution to their problem. Going back to selling cars, if someone said that safety was an important issue to them, then Chris would focus on the safety features of the car, and the benefits those features would have in protecting the prospect's family.

It's not that you don't highlight other things; you simply focus on the things that are most important to your prospect, while downplaying the rest. You find ways to give them more of what they want and care about the most. **It's all about knowing your prospect.** Your "head knowledge" about your product or service is only going to take you so far. Knowledge about your prospects, on the other hand, can take you as far as you want to go, because then you've transcended the actual products and services you sell. You've ascended to a place where you're selling to the person, looking for ways to deliver the benefits they want the most. **Focusing on the prospect over the products is a key strategy in any sales environment.**

CHAPTER EIGHT

◆ ◆ ◆ ◆ ◆

A successful business is constantly changing, developing, evolving, and growing! It's like a living organism that evolves to meet the demands of the environment.

◆ ◆ ◆ ◆ ◆

Grow and Evolve

A successful business is constantly changing, developing, and growing. It's like a living organism that evolves to meet the demands of the environment. That environment, or course, is the marketplace. **A business feeds off its market. It changes, grows, or evolves based on that market...** and it can even devolve and die, which is another story. We don't like to talk about the devolution of a market, but it does happen.

Life is all about change, and business is simply an accelerated life. You get more of the good *and* more of the bad; but either way, it's constantly in motion, changing in small ways over time—just like us. We can't necessarily see it in ourselves, but every day we're getting older. We do see it in people that we haven't seen for a while; when you only see them once every few years, you go, "Holy crap! What happened?" Well, what happened is life. We're all getting older, every damned day. When you're looking in the mirror every day, you don't necessarily notice it... but you do over time.

The same thing happens with your business. **Like everything else, business is always in motion, evolving into something different.** Now, there are some things in your market that don't change, but they're rare; most things do change, sometimes slowly but more definitely in the long term. For example, there are things that we sold back in the 1990s that we couldn't sell in the decade after that and certainly couldn't sell today, just because the basic boundary conditions of the market have changed. **The market is mostly the same, but different dynamics and technologies have come into play.**

You have to accept that things are always in motion, and take the changes—whether incremental or sudden—into account, rolling with the punches. Success in business is a moving target. **There is no one way to succeed, except the way of testing constantly and trying new things, keeping an eye on your competition, studying your prospects and their needs, and trying to keep pace with those subtle changes around you.** You have to understand the way that the market is moving and growing and changing. If you pull back a little bit and take a look at the big picture, you can see it.

If you're always testing, pushing the boundaries of possibility, you're going to find out what works best—and what doesn't work at all. You're going to find new directions to move in, some of which may be a little unexpected at first. You're going to stay on top of it, as long as you're innovative. As Ray Kroc of McDonald's fame once told a reporter who asked, back in the 1960s, what he planned to do about his sudden rash of copycat competitors: **"We will innovate faster than they can copy." You have to do the same.**

Your best ideas come when you're being innovative, and a big part of innovation is testing. You've got to try a lot of different things, because that's the only way you're going to know what works and what doesn't. You're going to find your best ideas come through that process of experimenting with lots of different things, and making subtle tweaks all along the way.

CHAPTER EIGHT: Grow and Evolve

Of course, you'll need to stay closely in touch with the biggest and best competitors in your market and what they're doing successfully, so you can model yourself after them somewhat — at least, in such a way that you're not just being a copycat. You're kicking their ass in your own way. **You're being competitive because you're doing things that they just *can't* compete with you on.**

Stagnant businesses usually die. Their marketplaces change, and since they refuse to evolve, they get left behind. Even technological advances can leave businesses looking back, scratching their heads. Think about where technology has taken us in just the past few years. **If you're still using ten-year-old technology and you've never adapted, if you rely on that as part of your profit stream, you'll probably get left behind in the marketplace and your business will die.** So you have to constantly evolve and use the new technology, experimenting with new ways to reach your marketplace.

Consider the music industry. Most decades are defined by particular music styles, with big leaps between those styles. Those occur because the music industry evolves rapidly and constantly. You don't necessarily see that from year to year, but it becomes obvious over the decades. That's how you get musical eras, like the 1970s disco era, and the distinctive pop era of the 1980s. Musical styles evolve just like living organisms, changing over time, and sometimes it takes a long-term perspective to see those changes, since they tend to be incremental, occurring a bit at a time. It's the same thing with business or industry. **You won't see them evolving much on a day-to-day basis, but when you look back on a 10- or a**

20-year history, you'll certainly see a difference. You'll see all the evolutionary steps that took place as the business grew and adapted to the marketplace and new technologies.

Your business *has* to be that living organism, constantly changing; which is one reason why, looking back at the last Way before this one, product knowledge is highly overrated. **I think that's another reason to focus on your prospects and your customers: so that as they change, you can change with them.** If you continue just focusing on your product or your service, all of a sudden you're going to look up and ask, "What happened here?" You'll realize that your customers left you behind. They're in the present and you're stuck still in the past, because you were so focused on your product that you forgot to focus on your prospects, and you missed the changes that were happening to them.

I think this concept of constant evolution also reflects back on what we talked about earlier, which is to step out in faith and figure it out as you go—because **if you don't just get out there, you really are going to be left behind.** If you focus too hard on making anything just right, whether it's your product or the technology you're trying to line up to back your move forward, then you're hobbling yourself. Before you know it, that product you were working on, or that technology you thought was going to be an integral part of your business, is no longer valid in your marketplace. If you wait too long to implement any kind of technology, for example, it may stop being widely used. Anyone remember Zip drives? Where are they now? Where are computer bulletin boards? They're gone, past, dead. **You have to constantly be looking ahead, toward the future. What's next?**

Where is your industry heading? Where are your customers going, so you can make sure you're there to meet them?

If you'll do that, if you'll look at your business in that evolutionary way, you'll be able to stay on top of your industry's evolutionary changes. Business moves fast. **There are so many things happening on a day-to-day basis that necessitate minor changes in your business.** If you don't make a sincere effort to keep up, then you'll miss them. But at the same time, don't let this concept overwhelm or worry you too much; certainly, don't let it get you down. Don't think, "Oh, I can't do this, because I can't imagine my life being that fast-paced!" This truth is, this is a lot of fun. **Looking for new ways to give your customers what they want is always a challenge; it's exciting.** Remember, the biggest reason you're in business is to make a profit. When you play the game right and consistently stay on top things, you'll win—and the measurement of your success will be the profits that are coming in. That kind of success is its own reward, and probably the reason you decided to be your own boss in the first place.

Don't let the fact that you have to keep constantly changing and evolving keep you from doing it; it's part of building a successful business. You've got to stay on top of everything, and like Steve Prefontaine, you've got to be determined to succeed at all costs. You want to be able to say to your competitors, "If you want to beat me, you're going to have to get bloody. You're going to have to try harder than I am." **You have to be willing to do everything you can to win—and a willingness to evolve to fit your marketplace is an integral part of that process.**

Adopt that do-or-die spirit and keep moving forward,

THE MAGIC PILL!

adapting like a chameleon as the world changes around you—
because your willingness to do that will determine how far
you're able to go in business, and in life in general.

CHAPTER NINE

People want to do business with people just like them.

People Want to Do Business With People Just Like Them

More than anything else, people want to do business with people just like them. Sure, they want to do business with "gurus" too; **but they feel more comfortable dealing with someone they perceive as a friend.** This is a very good positioning strategy, if nothing else, because we all want to do business with people that we like and trust and respect. Those people are our friends; and as with all friendship, there's a commonality factor in play—a like-mindedness, if you will. That's part of what creates friendships to begin with: you have something in common with the other person, and feel that they understand you and your situation, because they're in the same type of situation.

Those are the kind of people that we prefer to do business with. **Therefore, your job as a marketer is to develop friendly relationships with as many people as you can.** And when I say relationships, I'm talking about real, emotional bonds, such that people feel that they know you. **And, of course, you're doing everything possible to know them and what they want, and you're doing things that make you likeable.**

Now, all this can be hard to explain; you've all heard the old quote that a beautiful woman is hard to describe, but you know her if you see her. Well, it's hard to put into words the characteristics of a likable person, the commonalities that they share. And yet we all know people who have the power of sheer likeability. You can quantify some of their characteristics, though not all. They're charismatic individuals. They're personable. They're not always trying to hold something back. They're not perfect, but oftentimes their imperfections are part of what makes them likable. They project themselves. They care about you, or at least pretend to do so—I'm sure that the world is filled with people who are just faking it.

But with the most likeable people, you get a sense that they're *not* faking it. They're real. You trust them. Sometimes, people that come across as backslappers, overly enthusiastic, trying to pretend they're your best friend... there's just something about them that makes you pull back. And then there are other people who just radiate likeability without even trying. They're real, and you feel like you can trust them. That's the kind of thing that you need to strive for when it comes to building relationships with customers—**and as you know, the more customers you have and the deeper the relationships that you have with them, the more that translates to the bottom dollar.**

You're always going to make more money by having a large group of people who feel that they know you, because they like you, trust you, and respect you. They feel like you have their back, that you have their best interests in mind; they feel like you understand them. **People are just dying to be understood, you see.** In this fast-moving world of ours, a person can sometimes feel like they're just a walking wallet, just another mark or, at best, a number. They feel that nobody really cares about them, nobody understands them, and nobody really appreciates them.

I believe that this problem is going to get worse and worse as time goes on. But it's going to get better for you if you're the kind of marketer who's committed to doing things to show people that you do care about them, that you do have their best interests at heart, that you're looking out for them, that you really *are* trying to give them more of what you know that they want the most. **That will give you a marketing advantage over your competitors.** The more your prospects feel that they're just cogs in the machine, walking wallets in an overly mercantile world, **the more powerful it's going to be for you to develop that marketing edge where you set out to prove to them that you're one of the few people out there who really does care about them.**

Of course, they know you're trying to make money; but you're trying to do so with a service-first attitude. You have to make it clear that you believe in them, and that you that believe in their dreams. You're trying to help them get whatever it is they want. You also understand them: their pain, their problems, their fears, their past failures, and their current frustrations. **You understand all that, and you're really trying to look out for them.** These are the things that represent true friendship. If you're in trouble, who do you call? A friend. You call somebody who cares about you. If your life is in a bad place, it's your friends—the people who care about you, the people who love you, the people who will listen to you—who make you feel special.

The marketplace is filled with millions of people who don't feel special at all, and it's only getting worse. So I want you to consider all this. Think about it deeply. You've literally got millions of people who feel like they're nothing but a number, who don't feel important at all. **They don't feel special. People are dealing with that every day of their lives, so it helps to show your customers some love.**

That's the first time I've used that word, love; and realize that I'm using it here in a loose, general sort of way. But really, that's what I'm describing. You love your friends. You care about them, and they care about you; so you have to get personal with people. In so much of the sales material that I review, it's clear that the marketers are doing their best to be oh so professional and polished, so perfect. Everything is neat and clean and pretty and edited, and rewritten 1,000 times. When you meet one of these guys face-to-face, every hair on his head is perfect, and he's wearing a nice suit. His teeth are so white they blind you when he smiles, which he does a lot. You almost need sunglasses around these people! They're just so perfect... **and there's something phony about all that. There's something lacking in their sales material. It doesn't deliver the message that it was put together by a real person —** someone real, someone human who has a story of their own, someone who does everything they can to get personal with the prospect or customer.

There's a movie from the late 1980s staring Steve Martin and John Candy called *Planes, Trains, and Automobiles*. It's a very entertaining movie about salesmen. If you've already seen it, you know what I'm describing here, because Steve Martin's character is a polished professional, antiseptically clean. John Candy's character is anything but that; he's the exact opposite, which is part of what makes the movie so much fun. They play off each other hysterically. John Candy's character is big and fat, and he smells a little bit and tells dumb jokes. He won't shut up.

He's annoying as hell. And yet, he's the real deal, and in the end, he wins your heart.

That's part of what being likable is all about. **Don't put on any airs.** Don't be overly professional with your customers. Be their friend, and talk about things that you share in common with them. Out of all of the marketing secrets that we've learned since we started our business back in 1988, the one thing that's made us more money than anything else is just that—the fact that we're honest and real with people, and we've told them our story from the very beginning. **Our story is our customer's story, so it resonates with them, and always has.** There are millions of people out there searching for a way to make money. That's our marketplace. So Eileen and I told our story from Day One. We showed people our pictures; and, of course, we don't have Hollywood good looks or anything like that. We're regular people—the kind of people that, thank God, the whole world is mostly made of.

We've never tried to put on any airs with them; instead, we talk about the years that we spent searching for a way to make money. We talk about all the fears, failures, and frustrations we went through. We've never tried to hold any of that back; we've always put ourselves out. **And then, of course, we tell the story about how things turned around for us, and how we now want to help turn things around for *them*.** We earn their trust, because we've experienced many of the same things they've experienced, gone through the same problems they have.

It all starts with winning people's trust; eventually, you win their respect. Eventually, they start to think of you as their friend, somebody who truly understands them, cares about them, and appreciates them.

Somebody will always buy from someone that they perceive as a friend; that's human nature. If they have 10 different choices, they'll always buy from the person that they feel they already have a good relationship with. So while it's ultimately all about money (it has to be, or you wouldn't be in business long), **how you get that money is to become their friend. You try to understand them in an intimate way.** What are their biggest problems? What are their biggest challenges and struggles? **Once you've identified those, you need to get them to identify with you, to see you as a real person.** You're not trying to put on any airs; you're just yourself. Some people will like you, and some won't. **But all you have to care about are the ones that *do* like you; let the rest of them go.** There's so much less pressure on you if you'll do that.

When I was younger, I needed for everybody to like me—and I'm not trying to say that I've transcended that. I've always been a people-pleaser; I'll probably die a people-pleaser, and that's not always a bad thing. But here's what *is* bad: when you're so worried that you're going to offend somebody, and you want people to like you so much, that you put yourself under too much pressure. **You need to get past that to retain your health and sanity.** The older I get, the more I try to practice what I'm preaching here—and the less I care about what other people think of me. I'm trying to serve them, to give them the best that I can, and I'm trying to be me. If they don't like it, I don't let it bother me.

As long as you've got a service-first attitude—as long as you're really trying to help people and you're focused on serving them—for every person who's turned off by you just being yourself, there will be one or two others who are turned on. Those are the people who end up doing business with you over and over again anyway. **So if you keep the pipeline full of good prospects and keep your marketing message out there and just be yourself, you'll end up under a lot less pressure.** Just try to serve them, try to give them more of what you know that they want, and become their friend. Make them aware of all of the things you share in common, and let them get a feel for who you are as a person. It can be liberating.

Twenty years ago, there was nothing liberating about all the pressure I felt trying to make everybody like me—and man, that's murder. I'd never want to live like that today, so a word to the wise here: take a page out of my playbook. Be yourself, and forget about the people who might not like you. **Remember that people want to do business with other people just like them. Strive to find a market you have a real affinity with.** That's exactly what we did back in 1988. Little did we know that this simple secret would translate into making millions of dollars... and yet it has. **It can translate into millions for you too,** if you find a big marketplace of people who share the same kinds of problems, struggles, and challenges as you do—and apply this simple concept.

CHAPTER TEN

"I have a lot of competition, but <u>ZERO</u> competitors!"

— *Kerry Thomas*

Have Zero Competitors

This Way derives from a quote I heard from a man who's very special to me. His name is Kerry Thomas, and he's the general manager of my best friend's pest control business. Kerry started in this business when he was 17 years old—and he's in his 50s now. He's never worked for any other job that I know of, and he's been running this particular business for a number of years.

I helped my friend with the marketing for her business early on, when she first took it over in 2001; the business was actually started in 1975. They've got 15 trucks on the road. **I spent a couple of months driving around with the guys, doing the pest control work, talking to the customers, getting a feel for the business and trying to understand things, since you can't do anything substantial with marketing until you really understand all aspects of a business.** The company is headquartered in Wichita, Kansas. It's not a big city; there are about 500,000 people in the entire metropolitan area. And yet, at that time, there were over 100 different pest control companies in Wichita!

And so I'm driving with Kerry, and we're going around doing these different jobs, and I'm asking him a million questions about the business. For two or three months, that's all I did. In the course of one conversation, **I asked Kerry, "Don't**

you ever worry about the fact that you've got over 100 competitors?" And by the way, they aren't the cheapest company either: in fact, my friend's business is probably one of the top five most expensive pest control companies in the area. Now, Kerry's not cocky at all, but when I asked my question **he replied with real spirit, "I've got a lot of competition, but I've got zero competitors."**

I thought, *Man, that is the coolest thing I have ever heard.* What was really cool was the matter-of-fact way he said it, without hesitation. That was his attitude: "I have a lot of competition, but zero competitors." That's one of the reasons why that company has been around now since 1975. It's one of the most successful pest control companies in the Wichita area. And by the way: anytime my best friend wants to sell that business, all she has to do is make one phone call, and she can sell it for top dollar. Not only is it a very profitable business, but it's very solid in every way. **All credit where credit is due: she's a good businessperson, and Kerry is an excellent general manager.**

If you were wondering, the name of this company is Midwest Pest Control. **Its long-established motto symbolizes its attitude: "If you want the best, call Midwest."** That's been the one part of their marketing message that they've carried with them through the years. And they do think of themselves as the best. They drive the best, latest model trucks, and they're always squeaky clean. The workers wear fancy uniforms, nicer than the standard kind, and my friend pays for all the dry cleaning.

Kerry's attitude has filtered down throughout the ranks. They all carry on with that attitude that they're the best. Sure, they've got over 100 competitors, and they're one of the most expensive companies out there. There are plenty of "cheap dates," so to speak, that are always trying to undercut each other on price. **Kerry doesn't want to do that, and neither does my friend; they'd rather maintain their high level of quality. That's part of the spirit behind the "zero competitors" attitude.**

It's the spirit of the warrior. It's the spirit of the entrepreneur. **You always have to believe that you're better, and you always have to strive to actually *be* better.** I do my best to translate that concept to my own business—to maximize the quality of the goods and services we offer, and to live and project the "zero competitors" attitude. We're not saying that we're the best, necessarily, **but we're confident that we're among the best.** Now, are we perfect? Absolutely not. We have our naysayers and critics, people we haven't been able to please; we even have our enemies. But we're striving toward perfection. We're striving to be better every day. **We continue to do things to separate ourselves from our competitors who also sell low-end business opportunities.** All the business opportunities we've developed in recent years share some very important commonalities that separate us from the competition.

One of the most important things that we do, for example, is ask all affiliate partners, distributors, and clients to play one small but extremely vital role in our marketing process, by taking care of our initial lead generation work. From that point forward, we spend all our own money and every other resource that we have available to advance those opportunities. We have quite a bit of infrastructure built up, including over 25 full-time employees. We have a sales staff run by a real professional, Drew Hansen, one of the best sales managers in the world as far as I'm concerned. Of course I'm biased, but I love Drew, and I believe in what he's doing—and I believe in our sales force, our great shipping department, and everything else about our operation.

So our distributors do things to generate the leads for these money-making opportunities—and even then, we give them the guidance and tools necessary to do so. Once they've found the leads, we take over, spending all our own money and other resources to convert those leads into sales. None of our competitors can touch us on that, though a few of them may come close. Now, there may be some people out there who are doing a better job than we're doing—but I can't find them. I can look anybody straight in the eye and tell them, very truthfully, that I personally know of no other company that does a better job than we do with the kind of business opportunities that we sell. **It's part of our bravado. It's part of what separates us from everyone else.**

You've got to have something like that for your business, too. If there's not already something there, develop it. You may not be better than your competitors, so *strive* to be better. **Find the problems in the market and create solutions.** And by the way, that big benefit I just told you about, where we're spending all of our money on all the follow-up marketing—that's a huge benefit for our customers. **So many of our competitors are selling money-making programs where they expect you to do everything on your own: you take on all the risk, and have to figure everything out yourself.** Those opportunities are filled with all kinds of gaps and missing pieces. There's no support, nobody to call on if you're in trouble. You've got to do all kinds of things you really don't want to do, and it's difficult and takes so much time to learn, and it's so expensive.

We counter all that. We have an answer for that—just like Kerry Thomas, with the quote that I told you about. Kerry's got all kinds of ways to differentiate his business from all of the other ones in the marketplace. You have to find something like that within your business as well. **You've got to create it, if it doesn't already exist, and then develop it to its full potential.** That won't happen overnight, but if you keep it up, you'll get better as you go along. You don't have to figure it all out at once, but do try to emulate the best companies from Day One, and strive to be even better than they are. **Do your best to solve the problems that most of the people in your market are facing.**

When you do that, you can have pride in what you do. It's a great thing. Firstly, it'll make you more money, because people sense that pride. **They're attracted to confidence. That's a big part of what salesmanship is all about: honestly believing in what you're doing.** You've got to realize that, and take advantage of it. The best salespeople in the world are the ones who totally believe in what they're doing. So when you strive to be the best, and you take pride in what you do, you'll have that attractor factor within you. It's something that really turns people on. It connects them with you. While people do want to do business with people that are just like they are, they also want to do business with people who are very, very confident in what they're doing.

THE MAGIC PILL!

Confidence can be faked, but not for long. **People can sense real belief and real confidence, so you've got to build it into your sales presentation and copy.** It doesn't happen by accident. You build it slowly over a period of time, by striving to be the very, very best that you can possibly be.

$ $ $

CHAPTER ELEVEN

I LIKE DEBT...

Part of the fun is to have the constant pressure to meet your financial obligations.

The carrot and the stick are both great motivators... But the stick is more important!

$ $ $

Learn to Like Debt

Now, this one may seem a little weird to most people, but to be honest, I like debt. **Part of the fun in business is the constant pressure to meet your financial obligations.** The carrot and the stick are both great motivators—but generally, the stick is more important, at least for me. I suppose different people are motivated different ways; but for me, the problem with all this goal setting that the gurus recommend is that there's not enough stick to it. It's all about the carrot, and the stick motivates me more. **I've got to have that pressure; otherwise, I just get lazy.**

This may sound odd to you, bear with me, and I think you'll see the logic in this kind of thinking. **You see, the more problems I have, the more pressure I have; and that pressure motivates me to work even harder, to do more.** Of course, being in debt, especially personal debt, is just one aspect of that. But it's an important aspect; and when you study the most successful companies, you'll see that there are times when they're up to their ears in debt. Every couple of years, I try to read this huge book called *Behind the Golden Arches* by John Love. It sometimes takes me a couple months to get through it, reading a few pages here, a few pages there. At the moment I'm only halfway through my latest read, and I've been working on it now for close to a month. It'll be another month before I finish it... and then, two years from now, I'll do it all over again.

THE MAGIC PILL!

Now, this is an old book, currently out of print. I hope someday they'll update it, but they haven't yet. You can find used copies on Amazon.com, but you'd better hurry— because I'm buying all of them! So what's the big deal? *Behind the Golden Arches* is (as you may have guessed) the story of the McDonald's restaurant chain. Everybody knows that McDonald's is one of the biggest companies in the world: a Fortune 100 company, publicly held since the mid 1960s. It's one of only two large fast food restaurants that aren't owned by a bigger company, and it's everywhere. **But what people don't know about McDonald's is all the years of struggle that they've gone through.** They almost didn't make it a whole bunch of times. One of the reasons that they *did* make it is that they got themselves deep, deep into debt.

As with cholesterol, there are such things as good debt and bad debt. But regardless of whether it's good or bad, **debt is just a metaphor for a much larger overall philosophy that I believe in: that problems can be good things.** Being in debt is certainly a problem; in fact, most people stay out of debt because it's a *big* problem. But problems are good because they spur you into action—or at least, they *can*. Sometimes they just immobilize people. Sometimes people just freak out in the face of their problems: and they get all depressed and paralyzed. But if you don't let that happen to you, if you take charge of your thinking, then problems are good, because they spur you into action. And life is all about action.

In that sense, therefore, problems are life-giving. Think it through. It's not the problems themselves that tear people down, because as the saying goes, the same problems that cause some

106

people to break down cause other people to break records. **It's what you do in the face of all of this adversity, pressure, and difficulty to counter it that truly matters.**

I'm here to tell you that having an abundance of problems can actually be a very good thing. **As long as you're committed to trying to solve those problems, and you're striving to focus on the solutions, and then you're using the pain that comes from all those difficulties as a kind of whip to spur you on, then problems and challenges will help you achieve more.** When we talk about being spurred on, realize that a spur is one of those things the cowboys put on the back sides of their boots; they dig them into the horse's belly a bit to get the horse to start moving faster. That's where the term comes from. So when I say problems spur us into action, I'm really talking about something that kicks your ass just a little.

Many people fantasize about having a life that's problem-free. I do, too. In fact, that's the one commonality that all my fantasies share—and I like to fantasize. I've got as active an imagination as the next guy or gal. But all of my fantasies *are* just fantasies, because they lack the one thing that reality always has: problems. **Life is problems. Life is pain. Life is struggle. Life is difficulty— and business is an accelerated lifestyle.** You get more problems, not fewer. Some people want to get into business so they'll have fewer problems! Ha, what a joke that is! It's probably the biggest joke that I know.

Look: if you can't handle problems, and you still want to succeed in business, then you'd better get involved in a good partnership with somebody who can take on all your problems. Now, you *can* do this. There are joint ventures and other kinds of business partnerships where other people might take on at least some of the problems and challenges for you. **But in a general way, business is one problem after another, just as life is.** And with business, often the bigger you get, or the more money you want to make, the more problems you have to face.

Debt is one of those problems that a lot of successful companies have on their shoulders all the time, particularly manageable debt. However you classify it, it's pressure, and the pressure from all of our struggles and challenges can cause us to perform at a higher level as it tightens in on us. Benjamin Franklin once said that whatever is painful instructs. It's true: how many times do you touch a hot stove on purpose? We talk about the learning curve, the painful process of learning anything new. There's resistance, and you have to overcome it. If you want to get stronger, you go to the gym and start pushing yourself hard, right? It's the resistance against the weights or the weight machine or the exercise equipment that you use that causes you to become stronger. You're pushing hard against it, and that ultimately tears your body down... but then it builds you up to where you're stronger than you were before.

So it's not necessarily the stress that matters here, though I believe that stress has gotten a bad rap. If you'll do your due diligence, as I have, you'll find out that people who say that stress is a killer is wrong. Stress is not necessarily a killer. First of all, stress is subjective; one person's stress is another's boredom. **Other types of stress are necessary to keep you moving forward. When you get right down to it, there's no such thing as universally bad stress.** Some people can take anything on. Other people can handle very little before they start freaking out. It's all in how you process your problems, the meanings that you establish for those problems, your level of skill at handling them, or what you're willing to endure.

What is bad, though, is strain. Yes, problems are stressful. Challenges and struggles are all difficult; but you can overcome them if you have some time to recoup, to recharge your batteries. If you're working out at a gym, for example, you have to put those weights down sometimes so your body can recover. It's the same thing with your problems. **Constant strain is what really wears you down; it just grinds away at you, so you have to avoid it and give yourself sufficient time to recover.**

There really are such things as good problems. **Focus on the solutions and try to solve them, and through that process, you'll keep moving forward.** Some of my best work — my biggest results and best ideas — have come during periods of intense problems, where I've experienced lots of pressure. **You often get your best ideas when you're in the thick of it, when things are chaotic, when there are all kinds of problems and pressures all around you.** That's when you perform at your highest level if you're committed to winning, if you're a warrior, if you're trying to achieve and do your best. So you may wish for a life without any problems... but consider this old quote: "All sun makes a desert." In other words, there has to be a decent amount of rain in order to support life. If a problem-free life is boring, then who really wants a problem-free life? Not me.

Now, I may fantasize about it occasionally, because we all

need a vacation now and then. **But realize that the problems you ordinarily face are just opportunities for you to perform at a higher level.** You've got to adopt that attitude and truly believe it; if you don't, you're doing yourself a disservice. Face it: in business there's always going to be problems, problems, and more problems. So change your attitude, change your focus, and strive to solve those problems. **It'll lead to some good things.**

CHAPTER TWELVE

If your back-end business is strong — you should set out to lose as much money as you possibly can to make the first sale to new customers.

Your first sale sets up all the future sales... The only purpose of your first sale is to build enough relationship with the new customer to get the next sale.

Maintain a Strong Back End Business

Your back end business is all the business you do with a customer after you bring them in and do business with them the first time—and truly, it's where most of your profit will come from. **If your back end business is strong, you can afford to lose money on the front end, which is where you attract the customer in the first place.** In fact, I believe that you should be willing to lose as much money as you need to in order to make that first sale to a new customer.

Your first sale sets up all the future sales. **The *only* purpose of the first sale should be to build enough of a relationship with the new customer to get to the next sale.** This is something, again, that's a real secret, because most business people just don't think this way! My dear, sweet wife is one of them. She ran our business for the first 14 years, and without her, the business would have never gotten off the ground. I can say that with all confidence and with all due respect to her. She's smart and levelheaded. I lacked whatever it takes to run a business, and I'm still developing those skills. Eileen did a phenomenal job during those 14 years she ran the company. She had all the maturity and common sense that I lacked. I had to learn a lot of painful things in order to get where I am today. All kudos to her.

But Eileen and I used to fight constantly about this idea of going negative on the front end. **For the years that she was in charge, she forced me to do what we called self-liquidation lead generation—which simply means that the amount of money generated on our very first sale with a new customer had to cover our initial advertising expense.** For example, if we spent $1,000 to get a new customer, we had to earn back that $1,000 on the first sale. Eileen really held my feet to the fire, too.

We would have these weekly sales meetings in our home, and our staff would join us here every week—and I suspect that some of them just dreaded it. Maybe some of them didn't; maybe they thought it was kind of amusing watching Eileen and I fight like we did. I suppose it was like watching a soap opera with real people. Fifty different meetings every year times 14 years—and a constant fight. **Eileen took the conservative route, and who can argue with that?** Again, she did a great job. Some of the problems that I've had since I took over the company in 2001 she never had in any way, shape, or form. **If anything, I've been overly aggressive on too many things. I've been too wild and crazy.**

But look. As long as your back end is strong, as long as you've got a lot of customers and they're doing enough business with you again and again, then you can afford to go negative on the very first sale. And in my opinion you *should* go negative on it, as long as you've got a logical upsell waiting for them— something else to offer them after they buy, something that's related to what they've bought. **That's where you make your first profit: on the upsell, not on the sale of the first product.** And by the way, this is a secret that the richest companies use.

That was one of my arguments for 14 years with Eileen. I kept pointing that out to her, but she kept saying, "I don't want to lose money on the front end." She could never think about anything but losing money.

But when you look at it more holistically, in more of a big-picture way, going negative on the front end makes sense if you've got customers who are going to re-buy from you again and again, especially if you can make that first profit on the upsell. **So I say, set out to lose money, because it will give you the power to market in a more aggressive fashion.**

Your ability to market aggressively gives you a competitive edge, and the most aggressive marketers are usually the ones that win in the biggest way. You do that by being willing to go negative on that very first sale—so that even if you earn $1,000 from a sale, it might cost you $1,500 or $2,000 to get it. You're negative now, so you try to make your money back as fast as possible; you try to fill that gap. If you do that, it doesn't matter that you're losing money on that first sale, because it's an investment towards future profits. **Your job is to make those future profits as quickly as you can.** So, how can you close that gap and seal it up?

Here's a model we're in the process of testing right now. We have a $495 package that we're selling to brand new small business customers. Our most immediate upsell on the back end—meaning the very next thing we're going to offer to them after they buy this $495 package—is a $5,000 coaching program. In taking them from $495 to $5,000, we're willing to spend up to $695 to make every $495 sale. In other words, we're willing to go $200 negative on the first sale. We don't *want* to do that, necessarily, but we're *willing* to do so. **The more you can afford to lose on the front end, the more aggressive you can be.** This gives you the kind of power that a lot of marketers just don't have.

We're willing to lose a few hundred dollars on that very first sale so that we can then follow up and make that $5,000 upsell, and therefore make back our initial profit as quickly as we can. So as you can see, initially losing some money so that we can make more money on the back end is a sound marketing principle. **And let me tell you this: the one promotion that made our company more money than any other so far was a three-step sale, with all the profit on the back end.** This was something we implemented about eight years ago, as of this writing. First we generated a free lead: for no cost at all, the prospects could get information about this special offer we had for them. In the next step, we got them on a monthly continuity program costing $49 a month. On the third step, we followed up with a $2,500 sale on the back end.

More money came in for our small company than ever before! Here we are, just a little, tiny company in the middle of nowhere, and we had times when we were bringing in a couple of million dollars a month—more money than we had ever brought in all at once! Now, we've had plenty of months where we did a million in sales, but we haven't had very many months where we did *two* million in sales. **And the truth is, at the very beginning we went far into the red ink on this thing—which was part of why it worked so well.** We got very aggressive with it, and we were spending as much as $500 every time somebody committed to paying us $49 a month.

The barrier of entry was that low. Somebody only had to spend $49 to get our basic package... and we were spending up to $500 to acquire them as a customer. Now, we didn't want to spend that much money; **in a perfect world, we would have spent no more than half that.** But the world's not so perfect, so we were spending what we had to. Fortunately, our conversion rate was high enough to make a fantastic profit before the promotion finally ended, which meant that more than enough of those $49 buyers took our $2,500 package on the back end.

This is a secret that the richest, most profitable companies are using. Think about that. **As long as your market is big enough, and as long as your conversion rate is high enough, this principle can be insanely profitable.** You just need to be sure that you have additional, related products and services to sell to people who buy from you initially, and that you're working in a market where you have regular, rabid customers who will re-buy from you again and again. **If you do that, you're not going to have any real problems, and you *should* go negative on the front end.**

CHAPTER THIRTEEN

Nothing gives you freedom like having **a few bucks in the bank!**

Secure Your Freedom

As an entrepreneur, you need to have as much freedom as possible to live your life the way you want it, and to take risks. **Well, nothing gives you freedom like having a few bucks in the bank—and when I say "a few bucks," of course, I'm talking about a lot of money, whatever that means to you.** It means something different for everybody. Give a teenager several thousand dollars, and it's the same thing as giving him a million, right?

Now, as the old Beatles song says, money doesn't buy you love, and it doesn't necessarily buy happiness. But there's one thing that money does buy for you—and if nobody's ever told you this, I'm honored to be the first. **The *one* thing that money will buy for you is choices.** That can mean good choices or bad choices, of course; but in this Way, we'll concern ourselves with good choices, choices that can potentially lead to lots of good things, especially power and freedom.

When you get right down to it, money is really the great amplifier. As far as I'm concerned, if you're already a fairly happy person, money will make you happier. If you're a miserable person, get ready for more misery and unhappiness, because money will bring it on. If you're already a generous person, having a lot of money will just make you more generous. If you're a mean SOB, then you'll just become a meaner SOB. **In general, money just makes you more of whoever you are. But it does buy you choices, and those choices can lead to freedom.**

When I was still dirt-poor, back in the early 1980s when I worked the flea markets on the weekends, I used to have a T-shirt that read, "Talk is cheap. Say it with cash." I loved that shirt; I wore it until it had so many holes in it I had to throw it away. I still feel the same way. Money is good. Don't buy into this whole thing about money being bad, this spiel you hear from some people who feel so superior that they think they have to teach you about reality. **The truth is, money is neutral, neither good nor bad.** Money is a tool; it doesn't care who owns it. **It just makes you more of whoever you are.** That's all it does. It can bring you more happiness; it can bring you more sadness, too. **It buys choices, and it's the choices that can empower or disempower you.**

I love making money—but I don't necessarily love money itself. **I love all the things that you have to do to make that money; that's the good thing about it.** The actual money itself? It's nice to have it, and it's always better to have it than not to. There's that old Mae West quote that goes, "I've been rich and I've been poor, and being rich is a whole lot better." I agree wholeheartedly. The Bible says that the love of money is the root of all evil, and that may be so. **But the love of *making* money is part of what business is all about; it's a necessary thing.** It takes money to just stay in business, so you need to be fond of making it. That's a given. **So my best advice is, don't fall in love with money, but *do* fall in love with all the things you do to get that money.** And make it a game; make it fun, and know what money can buy and what it can't.

For so many years, I struggled financially. All I wanted to do was be a millionaire—so that I'd always have enough money to live on without worrying. And then my wife Eileen and I started our direct response marketing company in September 1988, with her running the business and me trying to run the marketing. Within six months, we were bringing in an average of $500 a day. That was just so much money to us—an unbelievable amount of money for two people who been struggling financially. When I first met my wife, she was working as a cashier in a store, making minimum wage. I had a struggling little carpet-cleaning business: and when I say struggling, I mean struggling. I made maybe $150 on a good day. I worked the flea markets on the weekends, but that was never all that profitable.

So here we were, making $500 a day. This worked out to about $16,000 per month. Then we met marketing expert Russ von Hoelscher, and he knew all the shortcuts and tips for making money using direct mail. He basically took 20 years of his knowledge and experience and transferred them to us, so that they became our knowledge and experience. **As a result, within nine months our promotion was generating almost $100,000 a *week*. We went on to bring in over $10 million in total revenue within our first five years.**

I'll never forget how I reacted when the money just started rolling in. Much to my surprise, I became very depressed. Ironic, right? And when I'm really depressed, I don't want to talk to anybody. I was really bummed out. Eventually Russ called me up and said, "T.J., you haven't called me for months. What's going on?" Well, I didn't have an easy answer for him.

That was quite a few years ago now, so I've had time to reflect on it, and here's the conclusion I've come to. **The reason why I was so depressed when all those things that I wanted for so many years were happening, when the money was rushing in just as I wanted, was that I thought that when I had a lot of money, things would be different.** I mean, the money was great; don't get me wrong. And things *were* different in some ways; for example, we could do all kinds of new things, and we could eat in the very best restaurants. Again, money buys choices, and now I had lots more choices. But it was still me looking back in the mirror every morning. **There were so many things that *didn't* change, and emotionally, I took that very hard. Somehow, I expected everything to be different than it had been.**

And isn't that really what depression is all about? The reason you become depressed is because you expect things to be one way, and they end up another way. **I had these unrealistic and unreasonable expectations that were all emotionally based, and I couldn't even explain it at the time.** I suppose I just thought that somehow the money was going to solve all my problems, and it didn't. Oh, it solved some, but it actually brought on some new and different problems to take their place.

But even so, money is always good to have. **Having it can make you more confident, especially if you have enough tucked away that you know that if the worst situation happens, you're going to be OK.** There's an old quote on the subject: "Money will not buy you happiness, but it will calm your nerves." So think about that, and remember that the joy is in *making* the money, and then using it, not necessarily getting it and accumulating it and letting it sit around in the bank. **Money is like manure, you see: it's made to be spread around.** You can't just pile it all up. You've got to spread it around, so good things grow out of it.

Just make sure that you get that safety net in place, so you're confident enough that you know that you can handle the worst kinds of situations. It's nice to walk on the tightrope, take those risks, and have a little adventure in your life—and it's necessary if you want to make real money. But it's nicer to have a little safety net in place underneath, so that just in case you do fall off that tightrope, you're not going to die.

CHAPTER FOURTEEN

When asking, ## ASK BOLDLY.

When Asking, Ask Boldly

Too many people are timid; they're afraid to ask for what they want, because they think they might offend somebody by being bold. But as a marketer, you have no choice but to be bold when asking for something, or you'll go bankrupt. Zig Ziglar's brother, the late Judge Ziglar, wrote one of my favorite books in my success library. It's called *Timid Salespeople Raise Skinny Kids*. I bought the book because of the title alone, but as it turned out, it's a great book. The whole theme is that if you're trying to sell products to make a living, you can't be timid. You have to be bold!

Back in 160 B.C., a philosopher named Terrence (which happens to be my first name, by the way) pointed out, **"Fortune favors the bold."** You've all heard that saying; it may very well be the one statement that Terrence is best remembered for. It's as true today as it was more than 2,000 years ago. Fortune favored the bold then, and it favors the bold now—and later on, I'll relate a few stories to illustrate that point.

Here's another quote I like. Back in the 1600s, an English churchman named Thomas Fuller wrote, **"Boldness in business is the first, second, and third thing."** I like that. Be bold, bold, and bold again! Sadly, there are so many marketers and business owners who are afraid to be bold; they're always holding back, because something inside them won't allow them to ask for something forthrightly. When they do ask, they ask in a timid way... and you just can't do that and expect to succeed. **One of the reasons why you can't is because there are so many aggressive people out there who** *are* **asking boldly, and often they get what they want simply by doing so.**

Let me give you an example. I'm 52 years old right now, and a few years back there was this commercial pilot about my age who flew Lear jets. His main job was flying between Los Angeles and Las Vegas, shuttling rich people back and forth, though he did other flights as well. Now, he was a good pilot— but he was just a pilot. Still, over the years he got to know these rich people he was flying back and forth from Vegas quite well, because they were regular customers. One morning he just woke up and asked himself a question—and it's amazing how questions like these can lead to answers that change your life, because that's exactly what this question did. The question was simple: *What's the difference between my rich regulars and me?*

By this point, he was on a first-name basis with most of his regulars. He knew them well enough to know their good sides and their bad sides, and how much of their public images were façades. They let their guards down with him. After some thinking, **he came to the conclusion that there wasn't really that much difference between him and his clients, except for one thing: the fact that they were all audacious. They just never held back! They weren't afraid to go for their dreams.** They were out there making things happen. They were far from timid. He was inspired by that—and not long afterward, he started a business with the help of some of those people. The company was called "Solo Flex"—you've probably heard of it—and he became a multi-millionaire in no time flat. True story! All it took was asking himself a simple question: *What's different about these successful people?*

There are many, many marketers out there right now who are very aggressive. They're not afraid to boldly ask for what they want. You can't hesitate to do the same because as another famous quote puts it, **"He who hesitates is lost."** Now, one of the great things about Direct Response Marketing, which is how we handle most of our marketing, is that **you don't face rejection on a daily basis like sales representatives do**— though the fact is, you still face rejection when you get low response rates. When not enough people respond to your offers, they're really rejecting it. And so, **you have to ask very, very boldly for what you want, even in your sales material.**

This is one of the things that's missing in a lot of copy. The writers play up all the benefits and list all the great things you're going to get if you buy, but they don't tell you loudly enough what you're *not* going to receive if you don't take action. **Part of asking boldly is telling people clearly what you want them to do and why they need to do it. But you also need to emphasize what they're *not* going to get if they fail to take the action you want them to take.** You've got to make it real. You've got to play into their emotions and expectations. People will do more to avoid a loss than to gain something—so you've got to make that loss very real to them, by telling them about all the great things they'll lose out on if they don't buy.

I'm working on a promotion right now for a new company out of Dallas, Texas, that has an amazing diet product. We believe that they could be the next Herbalife—that is, the next multibillion dollar Multi-Level Marketing Company. So in the sales copy I'm writing, I'm spending a lot of time telling people that I really, firmly believe that if they don't take action and send for this initial success package we're offering, they're going to miss out on something that could change their lives—and if that happens, they're going to feel terrible when this company *does* become one of those MLM giants. **I'm trying to make that pain very real to them, which you should also do with your own sales copy.** Tell them exactly what you need them to do and exactly what they're going to miss out on if they don't. You can't pussyfoot around; you've got to be very clear, and you've got to be audacious and aggressive, because you're competing with other aggressive marketers.

Like it or not, there's a certain level of unfairness in the marketplace. Part of that unfairness is the fact that it's not always the best product or service that wins. **Often the winner is the most aggressive marketer—the one who's the boldest.** So don't be afraid to be bold! Rejection can't kill you. All the great salespeople know that. You can't take it personally. **The worst thing that somebody can do is say no; and there's no way that can hurt you if you don't take it personally.**

Of course, nobody just comes out of their mother's womb bold and aggressive and audacious. **It's a learned skill, and it's something that anybody can learn.** Admittedly, some people are more predisposed to being that way—loud and obnoxious and kind of egotistical—but sometimes the boldest people are the ones who have a kind of quietness to them. They're not loud. They're not overly aggressive. They're just not going to take no for an answer, come hell or high water. Pay attention to the people who are getting what they want; the people who seem to be blessed, so to speak, so that everything works out for them. Do that, and you'll see that they've developed this boldness factor within themselves. All you have to do is model your behavior on theirs, and you can achieve the same results that they achieve.

Too much timidity is dangerous in any aspect of life. For example, here in Kansas, they just changed the speed limit on the Interstate highways from 70 to 75 miles per hour. And so now you've got people barreling down the highway at 75-80 mph — since after all, most people drive about five miles over the speed limit. Well, if that's the flow of traffic, then there's no real issue with it (in my opinion). The same would be true if everyone was going 90. But here's the rub: the minimum speed on those same highways is 40 miles an hour. Now, you might think that's a safe speed... but it's not, really, if everybody around you is driving 75 or 80. By driving timidly, you're creating a dangerous situation. You're at high risk of getting slammed into by someone who's going 80, not realizing there's someone going half their speed down the Interstate. At the very least, you'll have a lot of horns honking at you, and you'll get a lot of dirty looks. So regardless of what you think about people driving 80 mph, if that's the prevailing speed, you'd better do what everybody else is doing, so you can keep up.

The same is true in business. Now, I'm not saying you should just follow the crowd in every instance; that's not my point. What I'm trying to say is that there are plenty of aggressive marketers out there, no matter the marketplace you choose. **So if _you're_ not aggressive in your marketing, you're**

going to be like that car going 40 down the highway: you risk getting rear-ended or run over by other marketers who are aggressively going after the consumers in your marketplace. **At the very least, if you're not bold in your marketing, you're going to get left behind by others who aren't afraid to ask for the sale.**

I think there's a lot of power behind this concept of asking boldly, in every aspect of life. There's a Danish proverb that says: "He who is afraid of asking is ashamed of learning." People who aren't afraid to ask questions tend to be eager learners. They're hungry for information. **The bold ones in any field are the ones who are exposed to, and soak up, the most knowledge.** Timid people wait for knowledge — and in our case, business — to just come to them. The timid marketer doesn't take a bold, aggressive stance to his marketing, and so he misses out on sales. Similarly, there's a Chinese Proverb that says, "He who asks is a fool for five minutes, but he who does not ask remains a fool forever." **Sometimes, it's only the fear of asking that keeps people from action.** You've heard people say that there's no such thing as a stupid question. Though that's not necessarily true, the fact is that even a "dumb question" makes you look silly for a few minutes at most... and then people forget about it.

If you never ask, you never learn — and in our business, you never *earn*. And don't just ask, ask boldly!

When I think about this concept of boldly asking for what you want, I often think about Chris Lakey's kids. He has six, ranging in age from 14 down to 4, and he tells me stories about them all the time. Well, all of them are really good at asking for what they want. Now, Chris tells me that he sometimes thinks that with his 12-year-old son, he might say no too much. He tries not to; he doesn't want to be the parent who says no for the sake of saying no. If he doesn't have a good reason not to say yes, he likes to say yes. But he's said no to Austin a lot over the years, he says, and sometimes he sees some timidity in his son, where he's not boldly asking for what he wants. Chris always tells him, "Just ask! It doesn't matter if I say no. Just ask! You're no worse off, and maybe I'll say yes; maybe you'll get what you want."

Just a few days ago, Austin asked Chris if he could buy a new video game for his Nintendo DS. Chris could tell he was a little nervous; but he had some money saved up, so it was no issue. Chris just had to find the time to go to the store and buy it for him. But at least Austin was asking; and all kids do this. Even the ones who are timid about it eventually learn to ask for what they want. Chris's four-year-old asks incessantly for what he wants, and so does his five-year-old daughter. Sometimes she'll ask again before Chris answers the first request! And so he has to tell her, "Slow down. You asked, now wait for the answer," because she's so bold in asking. In fact, Chris has learned to tell her up front that she's going to have to wait for the answer, because she doesn't really accept the notion that she has to silently wait for him to decide something.

Kids don't mind throwing it out there again and again; they're masters when it comes to at least attempting to get what they want. But somewhere along the way, as we mature, a switch flips, and we become hesitant about boldly asking about what we want, and most of us just *stop* asking. **I think that hurts us in business, because it translates into fewer sales. To really profit, then, you need to flip your switch back to**

"bold mode." You can't skirt around the issue and ask someone how you can help them, or if they have any questions about this, that, or the other, without coming right out and asking for the order. **Too much money is left on the table because marketers and salespeople are timid when it comes to asking for sales.** When you're bold and don't fear rejection, your sales will improve just because you ask for the sale. If you don't ask, you'll never get a "yes."

Most of us are passive shoppers; it's easier to walk out of a store than to buy something. Even if you go into a store intending to buy, you might have only a general idea of what; for example, you might think, "I need some clothes," and go shopping with only that vague concept in mind. You're not really going out to buy a specific outfit. Sometimes you do go shopping for something specific, like shampoo, but more often you don't. But let's say you just want to buy a suit. Your concept is general, and you're willing to browse, to learn what's out there, and to be persuaded if someone pitches a particular outfit. Let's say you go to a clothing store, and you walk in and just browse. Again, the easiest thing to do is just walk out of the store without buying anything: there are too many choices, too many decisions to make. **Well, a good salesperson will help you get that clutter out of your head, and start walking you through the process of figuring out what you want and need.** They'll find out what your style is, maybe measure you to get your size, point you in a certain direction or to a certain brand, and then they'll get you in the dressing room to try one on. Pretty soon, you have a suit.

A bold salesperson will bring you to the point where the

natural conclusion puts you at the cash register, giving them your credit card, because they walked you through the buying process. They know you came into the store because you were interested in buying a suit, so they were bold enough to ask you what you wanted, and to make suggestions based on what you told them. Without hesitation, they've walked you through the steps it takes to get to the cash register. That's how it works in a lot of businesses; you could be buying a car in a car lot, or responding to an offer that you received in the mail and talking to a salesperson on the phone. **Whatever the scenario is, a bold salesperson is always going to do better than a timid one.**

Maybe you don't fancy yourself as a salesperson; maybe you just have a little boutique or a little corner store. Well, you still have to boldly ask for the sale, no matter what. If you're not asking your customers to do business with you in all your ads, and in the way that you handle people when they walk into your store, then they're going to buy somewhere else. **I'm not saying that you have to be rude or abrupt, just straightforward and aggressive.** You need to become good at walking people through the process of buying your product or otherwise doing business with you.

So when asking, ask boldly! Anything else is going to result in fewer sales.

We have a friend whom I did some consulting for recently. He mailed 3,000 lead generation pieces and got over 100 leads as a result—and then three buyers. He's done no follow-up marketing. I tried to tell him, "Look, you've got to go after these leads aggressively!" **He can't assume that just because**

three people bought, those were the *only* people interested in the product. That's obviously not the case; he's got close to 100 other people who expressed interest. Now he needs to ask boldly for the sale by following up with them aggressively, reminding them about the offer, asking them again and again to buy from him. You've *got* to do that, if you expect to succeed as a marketer!

As I write this, we've got a seminar coming up next month in Branson, Missouri, and right now Chris is designing a series of postcards that hit our leads twice a week. Plus, we're going to schedule some teleseminars for them. We're going to do everything possible to stay on top of these leads, to remind them of the upcoming seminar, to keep that pressure on, continuing to ask them again and again to come join us in Branson.

When someone has shown an interest and then qualified themselves for something you're selling, you have to stay on them until they buy or they die. That's what being bold is all about—and the boldest marketers will always succeed.

CHAPTER FIFTEEN

A person's greatest need is to feel appreciated...

You **must** make them feel important and special and needed — **without** appearing phony. This is very difficult. But the world's most successful people have mastered this powerful skill.

Make Your Customers Feel Appreciated

Everyone wants to feel appreciated, **so as a marketer and business owner, you need to do everything you can to make your prospects and customers feel special and needed—** *without appearing phony.* This can be very difficult, but the world's most successful marketers have mastered this powerful skill. And again, it *is* a skill!

So how do you do it? **First and foremost, you have to get to a place where you** *know* **that people are special and important.** And that's not a phony attitude, because people *are* special. **They're important in and of themselves—and you really do need them in order to succeed.** Everything you want in life has to come through other people: money, health, love, you name it. We need people in our lives, and all people are special. You know that when you're holding a newborn baby. You understand what an absolute miracle you're holding in your hands, as you look at those tiny toes and fingers and smell that little baby scent. You know the absolute miracle of life at that moment, and you know just how valuable a human being is.

But we sometimes forget just what a miracle a person is. **People really are special... and yet so often, they don't feel that way, especially in the business arena.** Most people come to feel that they're just walking wallets or walking purses—that the only thing a marketer wants from them is their money. They don't feel appreciated, they don't feel needed, they don't feel important, and they feel like numbers... like they don't matter. As a result, they're desperately searching for a way to feel needed.

Nobody does a better job of making people feel special than some of the big MLM companies. I've been around this industry since the early 1980s, and I've found that the companies that are best at it give a huge amount of recognition to their sales leaders, always handing out all kinds of ribbons and awards. They have ceremonies and invite these people to speak, and do various things to make them feel appreciated and needed as part of the group. They do a great job of making people feel that they're a very, very important part of a community. Pay attention to how these established Network Marketing and Direct Sales companies do that.

If you want to study someone who rose from nothing to become one of the most powerful people in the world, and who did it in a relatively short time, take a look at Napoleon Bonaparte. His story is incredible! He once said, **"My life was changed forever the day that I learned that a man would die for a blue ribbon."** He found out early on that people crave recognition. They need to feel special. The next time you see a military person in full dress uniform, take a close look at their decorations—all the beautiful colored ribbons and medals that they've earned. Recognition of that type works very well not just in the military, but in the rest of the world as well.

I was once part of a group of high-level entrepreneurs—people who are out there moving and shaking and doing major things, people who are multimillionaires—and a big, big part of that group dynamic was built on recognition. **The group made people feel special.** They handed out Marketer of the Year Awards, and had contests, and did all kinds of little things to make their members feel recognized and needed and appreciated. **As a result, those people were turning around and spending tens and even *hundreds* of thousands of dollars with that particular organization.**

This method works for all people in all demographic groups. Most successful politicians are very good at doing this. Bill Clinton, for example: like him or not, as a politician he did an amazing job of making everybody around him feel special. If you ever saw the movie *Primary Colors*, where John Travolta played Bill Clinton (though it was never officially *stated* that he was Bill Clinton) there's a particularly telling scene where he's walking down this long line of people, shaking each person's hand for less than two seconds. But during those two seconds, the person whose hand he's shaking has his full attention. His other hand is on their arm, and he's looking them in the eye. For that two-second period, he makes that person feel special. Apparently, Bill Clinton just has a natural ability to do that.

All high-powered performers in every field do things to make people feel special. And as I've said, people really *are* special. They really, truly are. **You have to believe that in your heart, because otherwise, you come across as phony...** and we've all met people like that. You feel sleazy when you're around those people. Their interest in you is so cheap and shallow that you want to go take a shower after spending a few minutes with them. These people are slimy, and everyone can see right through them.

THE MAGIC PILL!

The way to *really* make people feel special is to get it in your head that they *are* special. It's as simple as that. You have to recognize what I call the "miracle of life," and see just how valuable all of us truly are... *all* of us. Value yourself, too. The more you value yourself, the more you appreciate yourself, the more you respect yourself, the more important you feel: not in an egotistical sense, but in a very *real* sense. **The more you feel that within yourself, the more you're going to be able to mirror that and naturally respect and value other people.**

This is such a powerful emotion, and the effect it has on people goes a long, long way. It's a quality that's very endearing. Again, to use Bill Clinton as an example, he just had a way of drawing people in, despite his flaws and peccadilloes. **The best politicians have this kind of personal charisma, which I honestly think is impossible to achieve if you don't genuinely believe that people are special.** The best musicians are like this, too: you meet them, and you feel like they're taking the time out to focus on you. Now, Chris Lakey has had the opportunity to do some backstage work with musicians over the years, and he tells me that some of them were less than friendly. But many of them were really warm and friendly, so outgoing that Chris felt like he knew them—even though he knew that the next night, they'd be in another town making other people feel just as special! They just have a certain talent for making you feel appreciated, like there's some kind of connection there, even though there really isn't one.

I would assume that there are people across all industries that do that, but politicians come to my mind first; and I think that's because smart politicians know that their votes come from schmoozing with the public. If they come across as jerks, they're not going to get very many votes; and so they have, in many cases, perfected the art of making people feel special and important. You can go on YouTube and can watch videos of politicians giving speeches, and there are a lot of examples where it goes something like this, "Thanks for being here today. Before I start, I just want to give a shout-out to so and so, and over here we've got so and so with me, and I also see this particular person ..." And then, if they're trying to pitch some kind of big program, they'll bring out somebody who's associated or affected by whatever legislation they're trying to get passed, and they'll talk about them and prop them up and make them feel special. **People identify with that; even if they're not the one being talked about, just by hearing the story they feel some kind of a connection.**

Back in 2008, after Sarah Palin was announced as John McCain's running mate, she talked in an interview about her Down Syndrome child, and how she would be a sort of a bully in the White House as the Vice President for special needs children. This resonated with Chris Lakey and his wife, who have adopted four special needs children from China. Chris and his wife felt appreciated by Sarah Palin in that instance, because she was talking about something near and dear to their hearts.

When there's a connection there, when you feel like someone empathizes or that they appreciate you, it does resonate. It could take the form of accolades for a job well done, or simply something you care about that they say they *also* care about. Any of these things can act as a glue between you, generating a binding effect that often occurs on a subconscious level. You may not be aware of it, but it draws you to the other person. It makes you interested in them. **You've built a relationship there. That's especially critical in business, even if it's just a client/merchant relationship, and not a truly personal one.**

So a salesperson or a business owner who wants to do more business has no choice but to find a way to make his or her prospects or customers feel like they're appreciated. There are a hundred and one ways you can do that. For example, if you run a local business, you might have a customer appreciation sale; that's an easy way to show people they're special. The Little Caesar's pizza chain does this every Tuesday in some of their locations.

Similarly, there's a local business in my area that used to be great at doing customer appreciation sales, where they'd let you come in early to attend their special events. For example, if they were going to have a big sale on the weekend, they might send their regular customers invitations to come into the store the Thursday before the big event, when the store was normally closed. You couldn't just walk in off the street; you had to show them your invitation. Only then would they allow you to come in and shop before everybody else—when the inventory was fresh and at its best, and you had the first selection. This made you feel important! Well, they quit doing that a while back; and the last time I talked to the owner, he told me he was thinking about closing his store after being in business for 20 years. Hmmm, I wonder if there's a connection? I don't know for sure, **but I do know you have to stay in touch with your customers and show your appreciation regularly, or they *will* go to**

someone else.

You can find all kinds of ways to make your customers feel appreciated, to make them feel wanted. **What really matters here is sincerity.** Obviously, you can have a relationship and appreciate your clients without knowing each one of them by name; if, for example, you're a mail order company like we are. We show appreciation for all our clients in various ways, even though if we met one of them on the street, we wouldn't necessarily recognize them. **So it doesn't have to be a personal relationship, but you *do* have to make them believe that you really are grateful for their patronage.** Appreciation is a special way to your customers' wallets, if you want to think of it that way.

Make them feel that you genuinely appreciate them. **Strive to make each customer feel there's a special relationship between you, one that you don't have with just anybody.** The more you can do that, the more likely they'll be to choose to do business with you instead of your competitors... which obviously increases your bottom line and puts more money in your bank account. That's what this is all about, so find ways to show your customers that you honestly appreciate them. If you don't appreciate them, learn to.

Here's the general rule: **Customers go where they're invited, so you have to constantly invite them, make your marketing as altruistic as possible, and keep making them feel appreciated.**

CHAPTER SIXTEEN

The 12 Paths to Power:

1. **Know yourself intimately.** People tend to overestimate their chances of success and underestimate their chances of failure. What do you really want? What are your strengths and weaknesses? What are you best at?

2. **Be an information filter and a knowledge sponge.** Keep searching for the truth! Keep trying to figure out other people and WHY they do what they do. Greater knowledge of yourself and the world gives you a wider range of possible actions to choose from.

3. **Get it together.** FOCUS. Focus on what you want. Most people want it all, and they aren't very powerful.

4. **Live an upright life.** Honesty is the best policy.

5. **Take a shot.** If you don't play, you won't win. GO FOR IT! MASSIVE ACTION.

6. **Hang in there.** "Persevere, no matter the pain, persevere." — *H. Ross Perot*

7. **Pick do-able objectives.** Pick battles you can win! Don't waste your time and energy fighting losing battles.

8. **Don't make a big deal about being the boss.** Be humble. You need other people to help you win.

9. **Don't motivate other people to oppose you.** Don't make people any more jealous than they already are! Don't strip someone down and cause them to seek revenge.

10. **Put your adversities to good use.** Adversity can contain the energy you need to succeed.

11. **Calm down.** Open-ended desires lead to nothing. Be satisfied with what you have, AND THEN, keep pushing! Relax and enjoy!

12. **THINK WIN/WIN.** Empower yourself and help others get what they want.

The Twelve Paths to Power

I'm going to spend quite a bit of time and space on this secret, because it's got many different elements to it—twelve, in fact. **These 12 Paths to Power are among the most important principals that you need to know in order to succeed in both business and life.** First, I'll list all twelve; then I'll comment on each.

1. **You have to know yourself intimately.** People tend to overestimate their chances of success, and underestimate their chances of failure. What do you really want? That's a burning question. What are your strengths and weaknesses? What are you best at?

2. **Become an information filter and a knowledge sponge.** Keep searching for the truth. Keep trying to figure out other people, and why they do what they do. A greater knowledge of yourself and the world gives you a wider range of possible actions to choose from.

3. **Get it together.** Focus on what you really want. Most people want it all—especially entrepreneurs! But since they're not very powerful, as Peter McWilliams once said, "You can have anything that you really want, but you can't have everything." So focus on what you want the *most*.

4. **Live an upright life.** Honesty is always the best policy. This makes sense, but the world is full of liars.

5. **Take a shot.** If you don't play, you can't win. So you've got to go for it! Massive action produces results.

6. **Hang in there!** "No matter the pain, persevere!" H. Ross Perot said that. Never give up.

7. **Pick doable objectives.** Choose battles that you can win. Don't waste your time and energy fighting a losing battle. That was a painful lesson for me, by the way—and I'm still learning it.

8. **Don't make a big deal about being the boss.** Be humble. You need other people to help you win.

9. **Don't motivate other people to oppose you.** Don't make people any more jealous than they already are. Don't strip someone down and cause them to seek revenge.

10. **Put your adversities to good use.** Adversity contains all of the energy you need to succeed.

11. **Calm down.** Open-ended desires lead to nothing. Learn to be satisfied with what you've achieved, and then start pushing toward the next goal.

12. **Think win-win.** Empower yourself, and help others get what they want.

I'll start with NUMBER 12 and go down to #1. So let's

think win-win first. You know, some people think that business is bad thing; there's a lot of animosity towards success. People look at corporations and think they're out to get everybody, and that all their wealth is ill-gotten. They've got it wrong. While some chicanery and cheating is inevitable, **business is generally a win-win situation all the way around.** It's about some entity—an entrepreneur or a business owner or a company— having something to offer to people, and then people deciding that what they're offered is worth more than the money in their pockets. The most successful businesses are set up that way. **You've got to develop relationships with your clients where both you and they win.** If that's one of your constant goals, you'll be in position to do very well for yourself; and your customers will be happy because they're winning as well.

It just comes down to helping people, really. You've probably heard the quote from Zig Ziglar that goes, "You can have anything in life you really want, if you'll just help enough other people get what *they* want." **That's where your primary focus must be: helping other people get what they want, so that you can get what you want.** One of the reasons I love the whole concept of Network Marketing is that it's based in helping other people, while helping yourself in the process. You're thinking win-win. It's not just about what you can get from somebody; what you're looking for is how much you can give in exchange for other value. Business *has* to be win-win; both parties have to feel they're benefiting, or it doesn't work.

NUMBER 11: **Calm down.** Open-ended desires can help you succeed, but there are some people who take this to an extreme: very ambitious people who just want to rule the world.

They want everything! Well, sorry; you can get what you want to some extent, but you can't have it all. As a result, some of the most ambitious people are also the most miserable. **They're always wanting more, more, more, and they're not happy with what they have; so their ambition is a curse rather than a blessing.** Take those people as a cautionary tale, and take it easy. Just calm down, and decide what really matters to you.

NUMBER 10: **Putt your adversities to use.** Some of the best advice I ever got was from Robert J. Ringer. I've got most of his books, and in one of them, he talks about the fact that **problems are a good thing.** Most people try to avoid problems, because they're often painful; and yet, **the pain can spur you on to do good, important, profitable things—often amazing things.**

NUMBER 9: Don't motivate other people to oppose you. There's a great quote that goes, "Your friends come and go, but your enemies accumulate." **The point is simple enough: don't make enemies if you can help it.** Now, you'll have to accept the fact that if you like to be the boss and you like everybody to *know* you're the boss, some people are going to dislike you. In the workplace, people may conspire against you and try to cause trouble for you because they don't like you. In the business world at large, it just means people will avoid you. They won't want to do business with you... and there goes your profit margin. **So don't give people a reason to not like you! Don't give them a reason to be angry at you or to try to oppose you in any way. Try to be a friend to everyone.** You can't keep some people from disliking you, even to the point of working against you; but don't give them an excuse for it. Don't give them an extra incentive. Sometimes you'll make an enemy accidentally, but there's no need to deliberately set out to make it happen.

NUMBER 8: Don't make a big deal about being the boss. **Be humble. Most people dislike cocky, egotistical people. They prefer folks who are humble and easy to approach.** Those are the most likable people on Earth, whereas the most despised are those who make it clear that they think they're better than everyone else. They walk around with that smug attitude, and talk down to people. So be humble. You can still be proud; being humble doesn't mean you let people push you around. On the contrary, if somebody pushes you, push back. But don't do so thinking that you're better than everybody else. **It's not all about you; and sadly, a lot of people want to make it all about them.** We live in a very "me" centered society. So I think that the more intent you are on serving other people, while tuning down the focus on yourself, the more likeable you'll be—and the more sales you'll make.

NUMBER 7. Pick doable objectives. I love this particular Path to Power, because to me, it's all about winning the war. **Whatever your primary objectives may be, you have to be willing to lose some battles in order to win the war.** Now, I'm still working on this, because I tend to be rather defensive. It's been a big struggle in my marriage, in fact, because whenever my wife and I get into arguments, my natural inclination is to try to defend myself, no matter what. Nowadays I just ask myself this: "Would you rather be happily married, or would you rather be right?" Because you see, when most people argue, they just want to be right! Well, I'd rather be happily married, so sometimes I just keep my mouth shut and I don't defend myself.

THE MAGIC PILL!

Nobody likes a defensive person anyway.

On the business front, ask yourself this question: **"Would I rather be rich, or would I rather be right?"** Would you rather get along with a customer, or would you rather argue with them? Would you rather struggle to succeed, or would you rather make a profit? Don't think that you have to hit a home run or a grand slam every time. Again, you're just focusing on the primary objective—what you really want.

NUMBER 6: Hang in there!. **No matter how bad things are, you're never going to fail unless you give up.** I like the Perot quote: "No matter the pain, persevere!" Don't give up! Refuse to accept failure or any appearance of failure. Whenever you face adversity, whenever you're hit by challenges or drawbacks, just keep moving forward and keep plucking away. You're never a failure as long as you keep hanging in there!

NUMBER 5: Take a shot. **Take massive action toward your goals.** Try a whole bunch of things at once, then pay very close attention to what's working, so you can put more energy into those things. **Keep testing new approaches because if you don't play, you can't win.** I think too many people just sit back and wait for all the right things to happen. They never get in the game, so how can they ever win? You just can't score unless you're on the field, so you've got to take a shot. *Just do it,* as the Nike slogan says. Get out there and play hard, because you can't even score a single point, let along win the game, unless you're *in* the game.

NUMBER 4: Live an upright life. Now, honesty is somewhat subjective, at least in some cases, so I think your best bet is to follow Shakespeare's advice: "To thine own self be true." When you're true to yourself, you can't be false to anyone else; that's the flip side of that quote. **Live an honest, upright life where you're doing what you know is best, and you're not trying to hurt anybody.** Honesty is also the best policy in business, given all these scammers out there. Telling the truth can be an excellent marketing tool.

NUMBER 3: Get it together. **Never underestimate the power of focusing like a laser on what you want.** One of the greatest analogies I ever heard about focus is that when they teach people how to drive race cars, one of the things they teach is that you must always stay totally focused on the road ahead. If you're driving 180 miles an hour and you start to lose control of the car, the natural inclination is to hit the brakes. But race car drivers are taught not to do that. You drive your way out of the situation instead; you stay very, very focused on just looking ahead, at where you want to go; and if you're a skilled driver and follow the rules, the car will naturally adjust itself. You have to stay very focused on what you want. **Not what you *don't* want, not what you would *like* to happen, but precisely what you really, really want.** Remain totally focused on your goals.

NUMBER 2: Become an information filter and knowledge sponge. Question everything. **Stay hungry for new knowledge. Try to develop your level of understanding about yourself, the people around you, and what makes the world work.** The more you can understand something, the better. Recently, Chris Lakey taught me something on this point—though he may not realize it. You see, we're both long-suffering Kansas City Chiefs fans, and the Kansas City Chiefs have had some miserable years lately. But the fan base for the Chiefs tends to be rabid. For some of these fans, if the Chiefs lose, their whole day is ruined. Chris used to be that way, but then he tried to understand the game a little. The more he studied the dynamics of the game, the less he worried when the Chiefs sucked and they lost another big one. He was able to go on with his day unscathed. That's a minor example, **but I think that the ability to understand something is crucial to dealing with it. Always think, think, think.**

Again, be an information filter and a knowledge sponge. I think that that's a good analogy for business education. I recently replaced the filter on our air conditioner at home, and the old one was just nasty—filthy, dirty, dusty. The reason it was like that was because it was doing its job: it caught the bad stuff, not letting it through into our air supply. That's what an information filter should do for you. It should let the good stuff through and trap the bad stuff. A sponge soaks up everything; it's not that discriminatory, **so you need a filter working in association with it to ensure that only the best knowledge makes it through for you to soak up.** The ability to improve yourself—to learn more about business, about your own company, about your marketplace, about being a better salesperson and being better prepared and able to market your products and services—depends on your ability to internalize clean, useful knowledge about all those things. So you do want to soak that knowledge up like a sponge, but you also want to have a filter in place.

There's a new study out that analyzes the difference between the brain of a person of today and the brain of someone who lived, say, 50 years ago. Basically, they were asking the question, "Are we dumber today than we used to be? Has the Internet made us stupid?" They concluded that it hasn't. What it has done, though, is rearrange how our brains process and handle information and knowledge. For example, 50 years ago, a very smart person might have had a huge amount of precise knowledge and information in his or her head. They knew everything they needed to know, and their brain was their computer; everything was stored between their ears. Today, it's so easy to get information on the Internet that it's not necessary to store huge amounts of information in our heads. **What we've stored there instead is how to get to that information fast and easily.**

For example: let's say we need to know which Civil War general led the troops in a specific battle. Back before the Internet, we might have committed that fact to memory; today, we know that we can just Google him. Basically, we remember where to find things rather than remembering the things themselves—which some people may say makes us dumber. Other people argue that it just means we're better able to sort and process and manage data. **That's where the concept of the information filter and knowledge sponge really comes into its own: knowing what information you need to keep, and soaking that up, while discarding everything irrelevant.**

And finally, NUMBER 1: Know yourself intimately. **Be aware of your good qualities, your bad qualities, your strengths, your weaknesses, what makes you unique, and what makes you special.** When at all possible, try to delegate your weaknesses to those who can handle them better; otherwise, find people who compliment your talents and abilities. Too often, people don't bother to sit down and reflect on their own character. One result is that they tend to overestimate their chances of success and underestimate their chances of failure in business ventures. I think that's something you always have to take into account, though, especially when planning and executing your marketing—or you'll fall victim to false optimism every time. So when you're studying numbers, resist the tendency to think that things are going to be better than they ever end up being. **Don't just plan for best case scenarios, ignoring the worst case scenarios.**

Part of the problem here, I think, is that most entrepreneurs are eternally optimistic. It's in our nature to forecast success because, after all, that constant positivity is what helps us succeed in the first place. We're always dreaming big and planning for what could be, and we let those dreams get the best of us sometimes... and so we fall far short of the best-case scenario. **We underestimate the possibility of things going wrong.** Failure and success both come with the job; we've got to accept that, but it's easy to forget about the possibility of failure. **Therefore, you need to make a sincere effort to maintain that balance—to know your tendencies so you can plan for them.** That's an integral part of knowing yourself.

Ultimately, power boils down to the ability to act; the greater your ability to take action, the more power you have. If you focus on the 12 Paths to Power that I've outlined here, you'll end up light-years ahead of everybody else.

CHAPTER SEVENTEEN

The power of simplicity:

If you can't sum up your basic offer in one sentence — go back to the drawing board.

The Power of Simplicity

If you can't sum up your basic offer quickly, ideally in one sentence, then you need to go back to the drawing board. You've made it too complicated, and some people will be confused. Now, I'm not trying to intimate that they're stupid; they're just busy and overwhelmed. **The simpler you can make something, the easier it is to understand.**

I'll admit that a lot of our own offers here at M.O.R.E., Inc. are hard to sum up in one sentence. But we could sure do it in a paragraph! In fact, here's a little secret about us that very few people know: although we've been in business now since 1988, and we've done hundreds of different promotions and more than 10,000 different mailings in that time, **we've only used a few different business models—all of them relatively simple. And yet we've generated close to $150 million dollars in those 23 years.** When I say "models," of course, I'm talking about the basic gist of the offer—the way the offer is structured. Over the years we've had about a dozen; and of those dozen, only a handful worked phenomenally well. They're all very, very simple.

Let me give you an example: our Beta Tester offer. Nothing could be simpler. Basically, we develop websites; and when a website is brand new, it inevitably has all kinds of little things wrong with it. So we go out to our customers and prospects and tell them that we've got this huge block of brand new websites, telling them what those websites do and what makes them unique. Then we tell them the truth: that there are bugs in those sites, that they're not fully ready to go. **We need people to help us test them by letting us put them on the Internet, and if they'll agree to do that, we can make them an irresistible offer.**

We usually start out by giving them 50 sites for free, so they can inspect them and prove they're valuable. Then we follow-up by offering to give them another large block for a nice price; lately, the number has varied from 200-300, with an average of about 250. People like the fact that they got the first 50 for nothing, and now they like the fact that we're going to give them more websites at great price. **The value is obvious!** Now, something like that may require 30-40 pages of copy to really build up and tell people everything they need to know. **And yet, you can sum it up in a paragraph or two, as I've done here. Again, if you can't do it in a sentence, at least do it in a paragraph.**

As simple as this model is, we've generated millions of dollars with it. We've used it since the 1990s, so it's not exactly a new idea; but shockingly, I know of only one other company that's even come close to doing what we're doing... and they do it somewhat differently. They copied us a little, and they've been running their offer for years too. **This model is clearly profitable and it's about as simple as it gets**—which is why I can't believe that we haven't had dozens or hundreds of other companies copying us. It's just one of the great mysteries of life... but hey, I'm fine with having no competition, too, so don't get me wrong on that!

We've got another offer out right now that's working like gangbusters: It looks like it's going to generate millions of dollars as well. The first tests have been simply phenomenal! I owe Chris Lakey all the credit in the world for putting this together, though the initial spark of the idea came from Drew Hanson, our Sales Manager. Drew even suggested the title of it; but then Chris took that ball and ran with it all the way to a touchdown! It's our "Cash in 48 Hours" promotion. **Basically, we've discovered a way to generate super-fast cash.** Our clients buy into this special advertising co-op, we run that promotion for them, and then we give them a percentage of all of the sales that come in for each promotion they participate in. **We even offer a guaranteed income bonus, where if those leads keep doing business with us, we'll give them a piece of that money, too.**

Again, it's very simple. We don't even have a real sales letter to sell it right now. Chris presented it once in front of a live group, and then we did a teleseminar, and that's it—but we're going to continue to expand it. Drew came up with the idea because we have another model that's made millions for us: our Advertising and Management Service. Again, this is a very simple idea, and it's long since proven. **As a client, you can become a joint venture partner with us and buy into an existing business framework. Basically, you give us money, and we do all the advertising and marketing for you. Then we give you a percentage of all the sales we make. Simple!**

Now, although they use the same few basic models, all our promotions are a little different. We're always creating different advertising and management service modules, for example, based on different products and services. But the model is the same. We have a few other models that have worked very well for us as well. None of them are complicated; all of them could easily be explained in a paragraph or so.

You *have* to create simple offers. People are busy, and they're inundated with all kinds of marketing messages. They only have so much disposable income, and they're doing everything that they possibly can to hold onto it. **Consciously or not, people always go on the defensive when you make them offers.** That's an important fact to keep in mind at all times. **Remember, too, that when you're pitching to people, they may be looking at a whole bunch of other offers at the same time.** They've probably very confused, because everybody's promising them the sun, the moon, the stars, and the sky. **Being confused, they're on the defensive; and often this means that they won't buy.**

Even if they're not confused, they may be looking for any and every reason not to spend their money. Sometimes this is subconscious; often, it's a conscious decision on their part, a stubborn refusal. No matter what you say, they're *not* going to buy from you... so why are they spending time listening to your pitch or reading your offer? Who knows? **All that's certain is that they're looking for any reason not to trust you, so you've got to make your offers simple but compelling.** It all comes down to what you're going to give them. It's all about adding value upon value. continuing to stack it up until the offer and its potential benefits are worth more than what you're asking them to pay. **If you can prove that, and make them**

believe that it's going to work as promised, it's becomes hard for them to say no.

Recently, we hosted a seminar for a select group of clients. We spent the whole day together, and then I took them all out for supper and we ate a good meal together. Just as she was about to leave one woman said to me, acting completely shocked, "I've already got two commission checks!" The way she said it, I could tell that she really didn't believe that this was going to happen when she bought into the program. I just said, "Oh, that's great!" I mean, we send out hundreds of commission checks in a single month; so it doesn't surprise *me* that she got two checks already, but it did surprise her!

Most people are doubtful. They're skeptical. They don't believe anything you're saying. They've built up all of kinds of barriers to protect us from all the advertising we're hit with, so your offer has to build tremendous value to even be noticed. **In the first place, you have to tell some good stories to slip under their radar—their buying resistance—and then you have to stack the benefits and the value so high that the money you're asking for in exchange pales by comparison.**

This idea of simplicity applies to a lot of things in life. I was just discussing our Federal budget with somebody, and it got me thinking about the size of our government. I often think about how much better it would be if we could get back to simple government. I can't remember the exact numbers, but I heard someone say the other day that there are something like 90,000 words in the Bible—the book that governs a Christian's life. And yet our Federal Tax Code consists of something like ten million words! Simplicity is *not* a part of our Federal system, though it should be.

I don't want to spend too long talking about politics, but I do want to emphasize my belief that, in general, we could all benefit from more simplicity in our lives. This certainly applies to business... though to be honest, **I think that complication rules the day for most businesses, and that's why a lot of them fail. They're too convoluted, too difficult to understand.** Everything about them is complicated; big bloated government and big bloated businesses tend to run the same way. If you want a decision made, you've got to go through 12 layers of bureaucracy. Even if you get past the very first roadblock, you've got to go to the second layer and get a "yes" there. And you've got to get a "yes" at the third and fourth and fifth layers, and so on. You have to wade through all these layers of complex bureaucracy just to get a simple decision made.

The key to business success is simplicity, and that's especially true with the offer, which is where all the profit in a business comes from. **In order to build an offer, you start with a simple business model and then tailor it to the offer's needs.** From the very first, you need to ask yourself, "Is this a simple offer?" If you can't sum it up in a paragraph—or better yet, a single sentence—then go back to the drawing board. Otherwise you risk confusing the prospect, and that's the fast track to a "no." **You need to give them permission to say "yes," since it's a lot easier for them to refuse; in fact, that's the natural, easy thing to do.** As far as they're concerned, that's the end of the proposition. It's over. You might still pursue them, but that's a secondary issue to them. They've rejected the offer; there's no more transaction here.

On the other hand, if they say yes, then there are other things that have to happen. They have to prepare to pay for the offer; so they've got to have the money in the bank or the credit on a credit card. They've got to be prepared to carry through with the financial transaction; and maybe that's something as simple as buying a burger and fries if you're a restaurateur. There are other businesses that require more complex responses to their offers—so if someone says yes, there are other ramifications. Maybe they're saying yes to a monthly obligation or some other long-term commitment, like buying a cell phone. When you go into a cell phone company and want to pick up the latest model, in most cases that requires agreeing to a two-year contract. It's easier to say, "No, I'll just keep the phone I have." **Remember:** *saying yes requires other things to happen, so the easiest thing for them to do is to say no.*

That's one of the biggest reasons to keep your offers simple: so prospects are less likely to say no. **You want to make it as easy as possible for them to say yes, so you reduce the barriers and limit the ramifications of saying yes.** Here's a good example: Amazon.com's "One-Click" purchasing. They didn't originate the idea, but they made it easy. As long as they have your credit card number on file, if you just decide you want to buy something you just hit a button and *boom,* you've bought it. How easy is that? From the consumer standpoint, you have one of two choices. Either you say no and don't get the satisfaction of buying the product, or you say yes, click a button, and forget about it until two days later when the product arrives in the mail. And by the way, speaking of that—you can set up an Amazon Prime account so shipping is free on most items and they come in a couple of days! That's a simple plan, an easy offer. It could be a lot more complicated, and on a lot of sites, it is. I guarantee you that those websites lose money because of it.

The simpler you can make something, the more barriers you can remove from the "yes" process, the more likely you are to get the order. This extends to all aspects of your offer, including the actual purchase act, as I've discussed above; but it's especially important with the structure of the order itself. So again: If you can't sum up your offer in one sentence, or at least a simple paragraph, then your order is probably too complex. The easier you can make it for your customer to understand your offer and then respond, the more orders you're going to get. **The power of simplicity is in its ability to take a prospect from a no, which is the easiest answer, to a yes, which is usually the more complicated option.** So make it very difficult for them to say no.

That doesn't happen by accident; it takes some serious work. In fact, it can sometimes take months or years to fully develop a promotion. **With some of our models, we've had to go back to the drawing board and fix them occasionally, tweaking them here and there, strengthening them, making them as simple as we can.**

Just remember: Don't overcomplicate things. **People need it simple.**